AQA A Level Philosophy

REVISION GUIDE

Paper 2

K Lancaster

Relativity Press
188B Kennington Lane, London,
SE11 5DL

Acknowledgements:
Thanks to George Mavrodes,
Emeritus Professor, University of Michigan

ISBN: 978-1-912338-97-9

1 2 3 4 5 6 7 8 9 10

CONTENTS

Introduction 5

The basics 7

Premises and arguments 8

Deductive arguments 11

Inductive arguments 12

Abductive arguments 12

Criticising arguments 13

Fallacies 14

The exam 20

Metaphysics of God 29

God's attributes 30

Omnipotence 33

Omniscience 34

Omnibenevolence 37

Eternal or everlasting 39

Paradox of the stone 41

Euthyphro dilemma 43

Arguments relating to the existence of God 45

Problem of evil 46

Responses to the problem of evil 49

Burden of proof 55

Ontological arguments 55

Anselm's ontological argument 57

Descartes' ontological argument 59

Malcolm's ontological argument 60

Teleological (design) arguments 62

Paley's design argument 64

Swinburne's design argument 66

Cosmological arguments 68

Aquinas' first and second ways 70

The Kalam argument 72

Descartes' cosmological argument 73

Aquinas' third way 75
Leibniz's cosmological argument 77
Religious language **79**
Verification 81
Eschatological verification 84
Falsification: The University Debate 87

Metaphysics of mind **93**
Substances 94
What is the mind? 95
Substance dualism **96**
Dualist argument from conceivability 101
Dualist argument from indivisibility 105
Mind-body interaction **107**
Epiphenomenalist dualism 111
Property dualism **113**
Mary's black and white room 116
Problem of other minds **119**
Physicalism **123**
Behaviourism 124
Identity theory 129
Eliminative materialism 133
Functionalism 137

Additional materials

Specification content 141
Possible exam questions 147
List of philosophers 152
Set texts and further reading 153
Glossary 155
Index 172

Introduction

How to use this book

This revision textbook covers the entire Specification for the second year of your A Level (Paper 2). You can read it all the way through, but a better approach is to dip in and out of sections as you revise them, or as you learn them throughout the year.

It is a good idea for you to read 'The Basics' (p7-28) as early as possible, as the information contained within it is vital to your understanding of philosophical arguments, and the exam. The information in 'The Basics' section is largely the same as that in the AS revision textbook, but it is worth re-familiarising yourself with it as it contains essential information.

When a term is written in SMALL CAPITALS, you will find it in the glossary on pages 155-171.

Anthology and text translations

AQA provides a list of set philosophical texts (see p153-4) to allow students to engage directly with philosophers' ideas. Sometimes these texts are written in a style which students find difficult to understand and analyse, but you should not let the language of the set texts put you off studying Philosophy. This book aims to present the ideas in the Specification and the set texts to you in a simple yet complete way.

What You Need to Know

The Specification is your guide to what you need to know (see p141); you can be asked a question about anything on the Specification. It is worth noting that the Specification does not always give lots of details about a particular area of the syllabus – for example, the Euthyphro dilemma, the problem of free will, and the problem of evil are only mentioned as brief bullet points, but one of these could arise as an essay question.

Criticisms

Some criticisms are described on the Specification; these are criticisms that you must know as a minimum, as these can specifically be asked about in an exam question. It is useful to know at least four criticisms (or strengths) for each theory, so that you can utilise these in the exam. Knowing four or more criticisms per theory means that you will be able to choose which two or three criticisms are most relevant to the question being asked.

Philosophers' names

There are some philosophers whose names are given on the Specification, and you will need to learn these philosophers' arguments because an exam question could mention them by name. For example:

- Explain Immanuel Kant's claim that existence is not a predicate. *(5 marks)*

Many of the great philosophers wrote about a wide variety of subjects: you do not need to know all of their arguments – only the ones which are mentioned in the Specification. If you know other philosophers or arguments which are relevant to a question, you can still receive credit for knowing these.

If you wish to know when a philosopher was writing, or what their first name was, you can refer to the list on page 152. This list is provided for reference, to help put arguments into historical context. But you do *not need* to remember the life spans, publication years, or first names of any philosopher, *and you will not receive any extra marks for knowing them*.

Philosophers in this textbook are referred to by their surname alone (the only exceptions to this are Paul Churchland and Patricia Churchland, who are referred to with their first names and surnames, to allow you to distinguish them from each other.) Non-philosophers such as Charles Darwin and Alan Turing are referred to by their full names, and do not appear in the list of philosophers.

The Basics Overview

Premises and arguments

- Inferences and arguments:
    - How arguments can be presented
    - Types of premise
    - Antecedents and consequents
- Deductive arguments – conclusions which are entailed by premises
- Inductive arguments – conclusions which are probable
- Abductive arguments – conclusions which are inferences to the best explanation
- Criticising arguments – criticising the premises and the logic
- Fallacies – flawed ways of reasoning which you should avoid

The exam

- Question weighting and assessment objectives
- How the Philosophy exam differs from other exams
- Laying out arguments:
    - Precision
    - Redundancy
- Writing good essays
    - Introductions
    - Conclusions
    - Paragraphs

Premises and Arguments

Overview

This book attempts to provide you with precise arguments so that you can break them down and use them in the exam. Where possible, this is done through arguments set out as PREMISES and CONCLUSIONS. It is important for you to know what is meant by these terms.

- **Premises**: the statements laid out to form part of the argument
- **Conclusion**: a statement which can be derived from the premises
- **Argument**: one or more premises, leading to a conclusion

Inferences and arguments

Drawing a conclusion from one or more premises is called INFERENCE. INDUCTIVE inferences form an inductive argument, while DEDUCTIVE inferences form a deductive argument, and ABDUCTIVE inferences form an INFERENCE TO THE BEST EXPLANATION.

- **Deductive argument**: if the premises are true, the conclusion *must* also be true. This is a way of finding a conclusion which is certain, based on logical reasoning.
- **Inductive argument**: if the premises are true, the conclusion is *likely* to be true. This is a way of finding a probable conclusion, by looking at evidence or experience.
- **Abductive argument**: if the premises are true, the conclusion is the best explanation of them (an inference to the best explanation).

Presenting arguments

An argument consists of one or more claims (PREMISES) and a conclusion. Arguments can be presented as a numbered list of premises, and C for the conclusion; this is called STANDARD FORM, and is the convention used in this book. For example:

1. All border terriers are dogs
2. All dogs are animals

C. Therefore, all border terriers are animals

Where there are INTERMEDIATE CONCLUSIONS (an inference drawn from premises, which is not the end of the argument), these are numbered as premises but begin with the word ‘therefore’ to show you that it is an intermediate conclusion. For example, in the following argument, premise 3 is an intermediate conclusion:

1. All Yorkshire terriers are dogs
2. No dogs are birds
3. Therefore, no Yorkshire terriers are birds
4. All swans are birds

C. Therefore, no Yorkshire terriers are swans

An alternative convention (which is not used in this book, but is fine for you to use in exams) is to write arguments as a bulleted list. If you do this, be sure to use 'therefore' to indicate the conclusion.

- All Jack Russell terriers are dogs
- All dogs are mammals
- Therefore, all Jack Russell terriers are mammals

Types of premise

There are different types of premise; a premise may be:

- A statement of fact (e.g. the Holocaust occurred during WW2)
- A generalised statement / assumption (e.g. all people have happy thoughts at some point)
- A definition (e.g. vixens are female foxes)
- A hypothetical statement (e.g. if a person loves God, then he will act morally)

Premises may be explicit or implicit. The EXPLICIT premises are the ones the author actually writes. The IMPLICIT premises are the ones which are clearly being relied upon, but have not been stated outright. In this book, implicit premises have (implied) written before them.

The justification for a premise is usually drawn from evidence or experience (A POSTERIORI). It is also possible to find the truth of some premises without experience (A PRIORI), that is to say, just by thinking about them. These include mathematical truths such as 5 + 2 = 7, and ANALYTIC truths which are usually definitions such as "all bachelors are unmarried men".

Subjects and predicates

In a simple statement, there is usually a subject and a predicate. The SUBJECT is the person, animal or object that the statement is about. The PREDICATE is the information about the subject. E.g. in the statement "the fish is big", 'the fish' is the subject, and 'is big' is the predicate. There may be more than one predicate, e.g. "the fish is big, grey and slippery".

Antecedents and consequents

A CONDITIONAL statement is an if-then statement, such as:

- If it's sunny, then I'll wear sunscreen.

The 'if' part of the statement ("it's sunny") is called the ANTECEDENT. The 'then' part of the statement ("I'll wear sunscreen") is called the CONSEQUENT.

Modus ponens

MODUS PONENS is a VALID argument which is sometimes referred to as 'affirming the antecedent'. This means that the writer is saying the 'if' part of the statement is true (typically, the conditional if-then statement is the first premise, and the affirmation – saying the 'if' part is true – is the second premise).

Modus ponens states that: 'If P then Q. P. Therefore Q.' (P and Q are variables which can be substituted for statements). Here is an example:

1. If Sam was born in Canada, then he is Canadian
2. Sam was born in Canada

C. Therefore, Sam is Canadian

Modus tollens

MODUS TOLLENS is a valid argument sometimes referred to as 'denying the consequent'. This means that the writer is saying that the 'then' part of the statement isn't true.

Modus tollens states that: 'If P then Q. Not Q. Therefore not P.' (As noted above, P and Q are variables which can be substituted for statements). Here is an example:

1. If Tom is a doctor, then he must have a medical degree
2. Tom does not have a medical degree

C. Therefore, Tom is not a doctor

Although modus ponens and modus tollens are both deductively VALID forms of argument (if the premises are true, the conclusion must also be true), they bear a resemblance to the FALLACIES of 'affirming the consequent' and 'denying the antecedent' (see p16-7) which means that they can be difficult to spot for students who are new to philosophy.

Deductive Arguments

Overview

Deductive arguments may be invalid, valid or sound.

Invalid arguments

An INVALID ARGUMENT is one where the premises don't ENTAIL the conclusion (there's a problem with the logic – even if the premises were all true, the conclusion could be false.)

Here are two examples of an invalid argument (the premises are true, but the premises don't lead to the conclusion, even though one of the conclusions is true):

1. Vixens are female foxes	1. Socrates is a man
2. All fish live in water	2. All men are mortal
C. Therefore, foxes are vertebrates	C. Therefore, Socrates is alive today

Valid arguments

A VALID ARGUMENT is one where the premises logically ENTAIL the conclusion (if the premises are true, the conclusion must also be true); it would be a CONTRADICTION for the premises to be true, and the conclusion to be false. A valid argument may have true premises or false premises; if the premises are false or uncertain then the conclusion may also be false or uncertain.

Here are two examples of a valid argument (the premises are false, but they do entail the conclusion; one conclusion is also false):

1. Pork is a vegetable	1. All ducks are invertebrates
2. All vegetables are blue	2. All invertebrates can fly
C. Therefore, pork is blue	C. Therefore, all ducks can fly

Sound arguments

A SOUND ARGUMENT is one where the premises are all true, and it is valid. A sound argument cannot be refuted (the conclusion is guaranteed to be true).

Here are two examples of a sound argument:

1. Pork comes from dead pigs	1. Foxes are mammals
2. Pigs are animals	2. No mammals are birds
C. Therefore, pork comes from dead animals	C. Therefore, no foxes are birds

Inductive Arguments

Overview

In an INDUCTIVE ARGUMENT, the premises support the conclusion, but they do not logically ENTAIL it, so it is possible for the premises to be true, and the conclusion to be false. In a good inductive argument, the premises should make the conclusion fairly likely – ideally almost certain (though it can never be 100% certain).

Here is an example of a weak inductive argument:

1. I have seen two octopuses, and they were both grey

C. Therefore, all octopuses are grey

The above argument is weak because it is only based on two observations, yet it generalises to all octopuses.

Here is an example of a stronger inductive argument:

1. I have seen hundreds of swans, and they have all been white

C. Therefore, all swans are white

The above argument seems reasonably strong as it is based on hundreds of observations; however, there are some species of swans which are black, so the conclusion is untrue.

Here is an example of a really strong inductive argument:

1. No human has ever lived beyond the age of 140

C. Therefore, no human will ever live beyond the age of 140

The above argument seems very strong indeed, as it is based on billions of observations (indeed, *all* possible observations), but still the conclusion may not be true, as people may be able to live beyond 140 in the future.

Abductive Arguments

Overview

Abductive arguments are INFERENCES TO THE BEST EXPLANATION. This means that given the facts (which will typically be presented as premises), the conclusion is the best explanation for them. There may be other competing explanations, but the writer asserts that the conclusion is a better explanation than all the other possibilities.

Here is an example of an abductive argument:

1. I know I have a mind
2. I behave in particular ways – when a heavy object hits me, I shout; when a relative dies, I cry; and I can quickly construct new sentences which make grammatical sense
3. Other people display these same behaviours

C. Therefore, other people have minds

In the above argument, the conclusion is not logically entailed by the premises, but the premises do seem to make the conclusion fairly likely (but not certain). There are other competing conclusions, such as that everybody else is mindlessly mimicking my behaviour – but other people having minds seems more plausible.

Criticising Arguments

Overview

Usefulness of arguments

One of the benefits of a valid deductive argument is that the premises guarantee the conclusion, giving us absolute certainty that if the premises are true, the conclusion must also be true. However, their downfall is that they rarely tell us anything new; they merely restate the premises in a shorter, more concise way, as if it is new knowledge, when really that information was contained in the premises all along.

On the other hand, inductive arguments can tell us useful new things about the world, by making generalisations or predictions about future events. However, their downfall is that they can never yield total certainty like deductive arguments can.

Neither deductive nor inductive arguments can prove the truth of their premises, so it is always important for philosophers and students to fact-check the truth of the premises before accepting the conclusion as true.

Criticising arguments

There are two ways to criticise an argument:

• **Criticise its premises** (e.g. by arguing that one or more premise is false or questionable)	• **Criticise its logic** (e.g. by showing that the premises do not entail the conclusion)

You can of course criticise the premises *and* the logic of an argument. When you approach arguments you come across in Philosophy, it is useful for you to consider these two aspects of an argument separately:

- Consider whether each premise is (absolutely) true – if one or more premises are false, vague or questionable, then the conclusion drawn from them is equally problematic.
- Consider the logic of the argument:
  - If it is a DEDUCTIVE ARGUMENT, is it VALID? Is the conclusion entailed by the premises?
  - If it is an INDUCTIVE ARGUMENT, how likely is the conclusion? Can there be other possible conclusions from the same premises?
  - If it is an ABDUCTIVE ARGUMENT, is the conclusion really the best explanation for the facts? Are there other more likely conclusions?

Be very clear about what you are criticising. Write things like: "Premise 1 can be criticised because…" or "This argument is not deductively valid because…" This helps the examiner to see exactly which aspect of an argument you are challenging, and it will gain higher marks than one which is less clear about what is being criticised.

Fallacies

Overview

A fallacy is a type of faulty reasoning, and even the great philosophers fall victim to them sometimes. Some of the following are not logical fallacies, but all are flawed ways of arguing.

• Circular justification	• Masked man fallacy
• Begging the question	• Category mistake
• Contradictions	• Fallacy of composition

• False dilemma • Affirming the consequent • Denying the antecedent	• Attacking a straw man • Ad hominem • Slippery slope argument

Circular justification

This is where the conclusion relies on the premises, and the premises rely on the conclusion. This forms a circular argument.

Here is an example:

1. Dad says that Mum always tells the truth
2. Therefore, Mum does not lie
3. Mum says that Dad always tells the truth

C. Therefore, Dad does not lie

Begging the question

This can seem quite similar to circularity. It is when an argument is based on an assumption (often in the conclusion) which an opponent would deny, and the argument uses this assumption within one of its premises.

Here is an example:

1. We are able to study the mind using a brain scanner

C. Therefore, the mind is the same thing as the brain

This is an example of begging the question, because an opponent who believes that the mind is *not* the brain would simply deny that we can study the mind using a brain scanner. The premise is based on the assumption that the conclusion is true.

You should never use the phrase 'beg the question' to mean 'invite discussion of', for example: "Saying that we shouldn't eat animals begs the question of whether we should drink milk." Although people say this type of thing in conversations, it is technically an incorrect use of 'beg the question' and has no place in a Philosophy essay.

Contradictions

Contradictions can be relatively easy to spot in some short arguments, but in longer and more complex arguments, they are tricky to pick out.

Here is an example:

1. Everything has a cause
2. The universe has a cause
3. The cause of the universe must be uncaused
4. God is the only uncaused entity in existence

C. Therefore, God is the cause of the universe

The contradiction here is between premises 1, 3 and 4 (and the conclusion). If everything has a cause, then God too must have a cause, but the argument proceeds as though this contradiction is acceptable.

False dilemma

A dilemma is presented in the form: 'Either P or Q. Not P. Therefore, Q.' This is can be a VALID FORM of argument such as: "Either Rachael is at home, or she's somewhere else. Rachael isn't at home. Therefore, she's somewhere else."

However, the argument becomes fallacious when the two options presented aren't *really* the only options:

1. Either you support unlimited immigration, or you're a racist bigot
2. You don't support unlimited immigration

C. Therefore, you're a racist bigot

This is a false dilemma, as there is a middle ground between accepting unlimited immigration and being a racist bigot; they aren't the only two possibilities.

Affirming the consequent

This is a fallacy which can be tricky to spot, as it takes a similar form to a valid type of argument known as MODUS PONENS (see p10).

The 'affirming the consequent' fallacy states that: 'If P then Q. Q. Therefore P.' Here is an example:

1. If you have hit the TV with a hammer, then the TV would be broken
2. The TV is broken

C. Therefore, you have hit the TV with a hammer

This is a fallacy because the premises can be true, without guaranteeing the conclusion. There are other possible explanations for 'Q' (the TV being broken) – premise 1 lays out *one possible way* in which the TV could have broken, but it does not state that this is the *only* possible way, which is what is assumed by the conclusion.

Another way of saying this is that premise 1 lays out a SUFFICIENT CONDITION for the TV being broken, but it is not a NECESSARY CONDITION.

Denying the antecedent

This is another fallacy which can be tricky to spot, as it takes a similar form to a valid type of argument known as MODUS TOLLENS (see p10).

The 'denying the antecedent' fallacy states that: 'If P then Q. Not P. Therefore not Q.' Here is an example:

1. If you have been in a car crash, then you have been in a car
2. You have not been in a car crash

C. Therefore, you have not been in a car

This is a fallacy because the premises can be true, without guaranteeing the conclusion. Just because 'P' isn't the case (you haven't been in a car crash) doesn't prove that 'Q' isn't the case (you haven't been in a car). Another way of saying this is that premise 1 lays out a NECESSARY CONDITION for being in a car crash, but it is not a SUFFICIENT CONDITION (you can be in a car without being in a car crash).

Masked man fallacy

This fallacy involves the wrongful use of LEIBNIZ'S LAW OF IDENTITY, which states that if A and B are the same thing, then they would have the same features. The fallacy is the assumption that because two things *appear* to have different features, they are in fact different things.

1. Lois Lane believes that Superman is strong and can fly
2. Lois Lane believes Clark Kent is weak and cannot fly

C. Therefore, Superman and Clark Kent are different people

We can see this is fallacious because Clark Kent and Superman are the same person. Believing they are different, or knowing different properties of each of them does not prove that they are in fact different.

Category mistake

A category mistake (coined by Ryle) involves placing something into the wrong logical category, often due to the mistaken assumption that something is 'more than the sum of its parts'. This is best illustrated with an example:

A tourist visits Oxford, and asks the tour guide to show him around the University. The tour guide shows him the colleges, halls of residence, lecture theatres, and libraries. When the tour guide is finished, the tourist asks "But where is the *university*?"

The tourist has made a category mistake because he believed that Oxford University was something else over and above the halls, libraries, lecture theatres and so on. He believed that Oxford University was in a different category to the buildings, when really, Oxford University *is* all the buildings.

Fallacy of composition

The fallacy of composition is an incorrect assumption that because something is true of particular examples, the same thing must be true of the group as a whole.

This is easier to demonstrate with a couple of examples:

1. All the parts of the human body have a particular function

C. Therefore, the human body as a whole has a function

1. There is a reason why ladybirds are red
2. There is a reason why blood is red
3. There is a reason why London buses are red

C. Therefore, there is a (single) reason why *all three of them* are red

Just because various things share a feature – e.g. the feature of redness or of having a function – does not mean that the group of things as a whole has that particular feature.

Attacking a straw man

This is not a logical fallacy, but it is a poor way of arguing. It involves distorting or misrepresenting an argument (usually one you disagree with), and then criticising that distorted argument. For example:

Jackson argues that:

1. Mary knows every physical fact
2. Mary didn't know about colour vision
3. Eyes are used in colour vision
4. Eyes are physical

C. Therefore, colour vision is and is not physical

This is a contradictory argument from Jackson, because …

This is an example of attacking a straw man, because Jackson's argument has been distorted or misinterpreted (whether intentionally or unintentionally), and then the distorted version is being criticised.

When you present a philosopher's argument, it is important to adhere to their actual argument, rather than a watered-down or confused version.

If you distort their argument into something with questionable premises and/or poor logic, then you are not doing them justice – and you will lose marks for it. To avoid attacking a straw man, learn philosophers' arguments as accurately as possible.

Ad hominem

This is not a fallacy, but simply a poor way of arguing. An 'ad hominem' criticism means that you are attacking the person, rather than their argument. In Philosophy, we should stick to criticising arguments, rather than the people themselves. Here is an example of an ad hominem criticism:

Socrates argued that mathematics was innate, but we shouldn't believe this, because Socrates was put to death for corrupting the youth, and we shouldn't accept the words of a criminal.

Slippery slope argument

This is not a fallacy, but it can be a poor way of arguing. A slippery slope argument suggests that if we allow a small act, then we're stepping onto a 'slippery slope' which will lead onto bigger, more troublesome acts.

If we help paralysed, terminally ill people to take their own lives, this will lead on to other types of euthanasia, and we will end up with people murdering disabled people against their will and calling it euthanasia.

If we legalise cannabis, then people will start using it more, and this will lead them onto harder drugs, until they become heroin addicts.

The slippery slope argument is problematic because it isn't true that allowing a small-scale act will always lead onto the bigger, more troublesome acts.

The Exam

Overview

In the A Level Philosophy exam (Paper 2), you will answer 10 questions, consisting of 5 on Metaphysics of God, and 5 on Metaphysics of Mind.

Metaphysics of God	Metaphysics of Mind
1. Explain / what is... (3 marks)	6. Explain / what is... (3 marks)
2. Explain... (5 marks)	7. Explain... (5 marks)
3. Outline... (5 marks)	8. Outline... (5 marks)
4. Compare and contrast... or Outline and explain...(12 marks)	9. Compare and contrast... or Outline and explain...(12 marks)
5. Critically assess... (25 marks)	10. Critically assess... (25 marks)

Timing

- *Duration of exam*: 3 hours (180 minutes)
- *Total marks available*: 100

This equates to around 2 minutes per mark, though you will probably work more quickly than this on the shorter questions, and allow more time for the longer questions.

There is no perfect amount to write for each question; it's the *content* of the writing which gains the marks, rather than the amount itself. So use the table below as a *rough* guide, not a hard-and-fast rule.

Total marks	AO1	AO2	Time to spend	Amount to write
3 marks	3	0	5 minutes	2-3 sentences
5 marks	5	0	10 minutes	4-7 sentences
5 marks	5	0	10 minutes	4-7 sentences
12 marks	12	0	20 minutes	1-1½ sides of A4
25 marks	5	20	45 minutes	2-4 sides of A4

Assessment objectives

Assessment objectives (AOs) are the different skills you are being assessed on in the exam.

- *AO1: Knowledge and understanding*. You must demonstrate knowledge and understanding of the core concepts and methods of philosophy, including the use of philosophical analysis.
- *AO2: Analysis and evaluation.* You must analyse and evaluate philosophical arguments to form reasoned judgements.

In questions worth 3, 5, and 12 marks, all the marks are AO1 marks. This means that you are assessed on your knowledge and understanding of philosophers' arguments, concepts, theories and so on. In these questions, you need to demonstrate that you can clearly and precisely articulate the arguments in question; you are not required to input your own opinion or argument into these shorter questions. (If the question asks you for a criticism, then you have some autonomy to choose which criticism you will explain, but there is little independence beyond this.)

In the 25-mark essays, there are 5 AO1 marks, and 20 AO2 marks. This means that you are assessed on your knowledge and understanding (see above), but far more marks are available for your ability to analyse and evaluate philosophers' arguments. You will need to put forward strengths and criticisms of theories, weigh them up, and reach a reasoned conclusion. This requires much more independence of thought, and you are required to input your own opinion into the essay. See pages 147-151 for some possible questions.

Philosophy and other subjects

Many other subjects require students to write essays and to answer short questions as a form of assessment. However, the requirements of many other subjects are different from the requirements of Philosophy:

Many other subjects	Philosophy
1. Often expect you to write for almost the entire duration of the exam.	1. Does not expect you to write for the entire duration of the exam. You might spend up to a third of your time planning, thinking and editing.
2. Often expect you to produce perhaps 6-8 sides of writing for a 1.5 hour exam.	2. Does not expect you to produce 6-8 sides of writing; 3-4 sides (in 1.5 hours) may be sufficient to achieve highly if your answers are well-crafted.
3. Do not usually expect perfection and may overlook small errors.	3. Precision is valued over the amount you write; a shorter but more accurate answer can score highly. Beware of making silly errors which will lose you marks.
4. If a question asks for two reasons and you give three (correct) reasons, you do not lose marks.	4. If a question asks for two reasons and you give three (correct) reasons, you can lose marks.

5. Require you to write in "continuous prose" i.e. full sentences and paragraphs throughout (especially in essays). (Ensure you check these guidelines with your other subjects.)	5. Essays should consist primarily of continuous prose, but bulleted or numbered lists, flowcharts or diagrams are permitted (and even encouraged) within essays, or as an entire response to a shorter question. This is particularly true if a list or diagram is the most precise way to present an argument (see below).

Laying out answers

Consider these different ways in which you could answer the following question:

- Explain St. Anselm's ontological argument. *(5 marks)*

Response 1:

St. Anselm put forward an ontological argument which shows that God must exist. This is because God is the greatest thing by definition, but if he was just in the mind then he would be less perfect than a God which exists in reality *and* the mind, so this shows God must exist in reality (and the mind).

Response 2:

1. God is the greatest being ("that than which nothing greater can be conceived")
2. It is greater to exist in reality as well as in the mind, rather than merely in the mind

C. Therefore, God exists in reality as well as in the mind

Response 3:

God is the greatest being ("that than which nothing greater can be conceived")	→	It is greater to exist in reality as well as in the mind, rather than merely in the mind	→	God exists in reality as well as in the mind

The three responses above are all saying similar things, but the second and third responses are more precise.

Precision

Precision is very important in the Philosophy exam, and the mark schemes make frequent references to it; it is particularly important in the shorter (3, 5, and 12 mark) questions.

Examiners use the word "precision" to mean being accurate (getting the wording exactly correct) and being concise (keeping to the point and not waffling). The aim is that your answers are correct, clear, succinct, you 'hit the nail on the head', and you avoid vagueness and 'waffle'.

Consider Response 4 to the same question as above; it is *not* precise, and would lose some marks compared to responses 2 and 3 above.

Response 4:

Anselm put forward an ontological argument which demonstrates our belief in God. He said that God doesn't just exist in reality, he exists in the mind as well, because existing in reality and the mind is better than only existing in reality. So this is why we believe in God, because he exists in our minds too, and the more minds he exists in, the greater and more perfect he is. This shows why we believe in God as the argument is really valid.

There are numerous problems with Response 4, where the writer has been vague and hasn't clearly answered the question. For example, an ontological argument is not intended to demonstrate our *belief* in God, but rather, to demonstrate God's existence. Further confusion is added by the suggestion that God's perfection is increased when more people believe in him; Anselm did not argue this. The final comment that the argument is 'really valid' is also confused; an argument is either valid or it is not. If someone who had never studied Philosophy were to read Response 4, they would still not really understand Anselm's ontological argument, because Response 4 is confused rather than precise.

Redundancy

If you have accurately answered the question, then simply adding more information isn't automatically going to improve your answer – in fact, it may detract from it, as the extra material may be redundant.

The mark schemes use the word "redundancy" to refer to irrelevant or unnecessary information in an exam response. Redundancy can demonstrate uncertainty, and should therefore be avoided as it can lose you marks. Consider this response to the same question as above:

Response 5:

Anselm states that God is the greatest being ("that than which nothing greater can be conceived"), and it is greater to exist in reality as well as in the mind, rather than merely in the mind. He concludes that God exists in reality as well as in the mind. God is an unmoved mover – this means that things in the universe are in motion, and something must have set them in motion, and that something is of course God: he is the first cause of everything as he designed and created the universe. We can tell he designed it because everything works so well, like a watch. This proves God exists in reality and not just the mind.

This is not a good response because all of the material from "God is an unmoved mover..." onwards is redundant. The response explains Anselm's ontological argument – but it also (briefly) explains a cosmological argument, and it mentions an argument from design. This gives the impression that the candidate does not really know what Anselm's ontological argument is, and they are simply trying to write lots of things in the hope that one of them is right. The response would score more highly if the material from "God is an unmoved mover ..." onwards were omitted.

Some GCSE and A Level mark schemes will award full marks if the correct answer appears in amongst irrelevant material. But it is perfectly reasonable to award a lower mark to a candidate who is uncertain of the answer, and a higher mark to one who gives the right answer but nothing more. If someone asked the question: "What is 3 + 4?" and person A responded by saying: "Six, seven, eight, nine" and person B responded by saying "Seven," then it would seem fair that person B gets more credit for their answer than person A. This is how the Philosophy exam works.

If you are thinking of including extra information which doesn't help to clarify or support your answer, then it is probably best to omit it: this applies to questions worth 3, 5 and 12 marks in particular.

25 mark essays

With the 25 mark essays there is more room for manoeuvre than with the shorter questions. Of course, if an entire paragraph is irrelevant then it should be omitted; however, being concise is less of an issue, as you will be writing far more. It is important for your arguments to be supported by examples or evidence, rather than being mere assertions.

As noted on p22, you should mostly write in continuous prose, but it is acceptable to lay out an argument in STANDARD FORM within your essay.

What's important

The mark schemes note that the best essays are ones where...

"The student argues with clear intent throughout and the logic of the argument is sustained. The student demonstrates detailed and precise understanding throughout. The conclusion is clear, with the arguments in support of it stated precisely, integrated coherently and robustly defended. Arguments and counter-arguments are stated in their strongest forms. Reasoned judgements are made, on an ongoing basis and overall, about the weight to be given to each argument. Crucial arguments are clearly identified against less crucial ones. Philosophical language is used precisely throughout."

But what does this all mean?

- "Arguing with clear intent" and "the logic is sustained" means that you need to clearly argue for one position or another. In most cases, it doesn't matter which side of a debate you argue in favour of – it only matters that you clearly argue for one particular side of the debate. For example, you could argue that the problem of evil demonstrates the non-existence of God, or you could argue that a loving God can coexist with evil. If you are not sure which side to argue in favour of, then simply pick one side and argue for it – never have an argument which is vague or indecisive.
- "Arguments are stated precisely and integrated coherently" means that arguments are explained very clearly, and that you comment upon them and show why they support your overall argument.
- "Arguments are stated in their strongest form" means that you must not ATTACK A STRAW MAN (see p18). Always present an opponent's argument strongly, rather than misinterpreting them in order to criticise them.
- "Reasoned judgements are made ... about the weight to be given to each argument" and "crucial arguments are clearly identified" means that it is not sufficient to merely explain a strength or criticism – you must also comment on how strong the strength or criticism is. You should highlight whether a criticism is only a small problem for the theory in question, or whether it renders it wholly unworkable.
- "Philosophical language" means that where possible, you should use key terms (see p155-71).

Introductions and conclusions

Your 25-mark essays should argue towards a clear conclusion. You should always outline your conclusion in the introduction – this isn't a movie; your essay doesn't need a surprise ending! Ideally, the introduction and conclusion should 'mirror' each other – i.e. they should closely resemble one another, and can even use similar wording.

A poor conclusion is one which doesn't really answer the question, or one which concludes that it's all a matter of opinion and people can believe whatever they want to believe. Below are some examples of introductions and conclusions:

Poor introduction:	**Good introduction:**
In this essay I will assess substance dualism, and I will compare it with materialism and property dualism. I will consider arguments for and against each side, and reach a conclusion.	In this essay I will argue that the substance dualist claim that the mind is a non-physical substance is flawed and implausible, due to the inability to explain how a non-physical entity could interact with the physical world.
Poor conclusion:	**Good conclusion:**
In this essay I have evaluated substance dualism. I have shown that there are arguments for dualism and arguments against it, such as the idea that we could exist without a body, and how a non-physical substance couldn't interact with the physical world. Both theories have their strengths and weaknesses – we might never know which theory is correct, and there'll always be a difference of opinion.	In this essay I have examined the substance dualist claim that the mind is a non-physical substance, and demonstrated that such a claim is flawed and implausible. I acknowledged that although we can conceive of a mind without a body, substance dualists cannot explain how a non-physical entity could interact with the physical world, and that is sufficient to demonstrate that the mind cannot be a non-physical substance.

It should be clear from the phrasing used in the essay – particularly the introduction and the conclusion – exactly what question is being answered. Hopefully when you read the good introduction and good conclusion above, you can spot that the question being answered is "Critically assess the substance dualist claim that the mind is a non-physical substance". You can tell this because the words from the question are used in the answer; this helps to demonstrate to the examiner that you are actually answering the question.

The poor introduction and conclusion are vague and noncommittal, and it is not really clear what question is being answered, nor what answer the student is trying to give.

The middle part of essays

Of course, you need more than just a good introduction and conclusion – the middle part of an essay also needs to be good. You need to explain theories, but you should devote most of your time to evaluation. You should prioritise depth of evaluation over breadth: the best approach is to cover no more than three evaluative points, but to cover these in depth – you could cover just two evaluative points if you wish to discuss one or more lengthy replies. Do not try to shoehorn eight simplistic and undeveloped evaluative points into your essay; this will not achieve a good mark.

Where possible, use key terms (see p155-171) as it will help to make your argument more precise. You should link each paragraph to the question (ideally using words from the question) so it is clear how that paragraph helps to answer the question. Remember also to comment on how crucial the criticism is (see p25).

Poor paragraph	**Good paragraph**
Philosophers point out that we can think of a mind without a body, for example, after death. This shows that mind and body or brain are not the same thing. If they were the same thing then something that is true about the mind would be true about the brain. However, we can respond that Lois Lane can imagine Clark Kent dying, but not Superman, when really Clark Kent is Superman. So maybe the mind is the brain too.	Substance dualists such as Descartes point out that it is possible to conceive of a mind without a body/brain (the 'argument from conceivability'). For example, it is possible to imagine a mind surviving after the death of the body. This supposedly shows that the mind and the brain are different substances. Leibniz's Law states that if A and B are the same thing, then whatever is true of A is true of B. If we can conceive of the mind existing while the brain has been destroyed, this supposedly shows that the mind is not the brain (and the mind is non-physical). However, this claim is known as the masked man fallacy, and does not harm the physicalists' argument at all. The masked man fallacy points out that just because Lois Lane can conceive of Clark Kent dying while Superman lives on, this does not prove that they are distinct: it is possible to conceive of two things as being distinct, when in fact they are one and the same thing. This can be true of the mind: just because we can conceive of a mind without a brain does not prove that the mind is non-physical.

The good paragraph has accurately used terms such as 'the argument from conceivability', 'Leibniz's Law' and the 'masked man fallacy' which help to demonstrate understanding, and they make the answer more precise. By contrast, the poor paragraph has used vague and confused terms such which do not demonstrate that the person has studied philosophy.

The good paragraph has also commented on the strength of the criticism ("...does not harm the physicalists' argument at all"), but the poor paragraph has not indicated whether the criticism is a strong one or a weak one. The poor paragraph also fails to show the relevance of the Superman reference; instead, they have just left the reader to work it out for themselves.

It is never a good technique to leave it to the examiner to 'fill in the blanks'; the examiner will of course be able to tell whether your criticism is a strong one or a weak one, and will know the relevance of the examples, but you need demonstrate that *you* know these things. If you don't write it, the examiner will assume you don't know it.

Metaphysics of God Overview

God's attributes

- God as omnipotent, omniscient, omnibenevolent, eternal, everlasting
- Incoherence of God's attributes, including:
  - Paradox of the stone
  - Euthyphro dilemma
  - Human free will
  - Other problems of compatibility

Problem of evil

- Problem of evil, including:
  - Natural evil and moral evil
- Theodicies and other responses including:
  - Free will defence (Plantinga)
  - Soul-making defence (Hick)

Arguments for the existence of God

- Ontological arguments by Anselm, Descartes, and Malcolm
  - Criticisms from Gaunilo, Kant, and the empiricists
- Teleological (design) arguments by Hume, Paley, and Swinburne
  - Criticisms from Hume and Paley
  - Alternative explanations for apparent order
- Cosmological arguments from Aquinas, Descartes, Leibniz, and the Kalam argument
  - Criticisms from Hume and Russell
  - Alternative explanations for the existence of the universe

Religious Language

- Cognitivism and non-cognitivism regarding religious language
- Verification by Ayer and the Vienna Circle
  - Eschatological verification
- Falsification and the 'University debate'
  - The invisible gardener (Flew)
  - The partisan (Mitchell)
  - Bliks and the lunatic student (Hare)

God's Attributes

Overview

There are different claims about what God's attributes are. For this module, you need to study five different attributes which are most commonly ascribed to God. The suggestion is that God is:

- OMNIPOTENT (all powerful)
- OMNISCIENT (all-seeing)
- OMNIBENEVOLENT (supremely good)
- Either ETERNAL (he exists outside of time) or EVERLASTING (he exists within time and lasts forever)

Other possible attributes

God is sometimes said to have other attributes as well. Some common suggestions are that God is:

- OMNIPRESENT (he is everywhere)
- IMMUTABLE (he doesn't change)
- ASEITIC (he doesn't depend on anything for his existence)
- Holy (he cannot sin)
- IMMATERIAL / INCORPOREAL (he is without physical form)
- Mysterious (he only reveals particular information to humans)
- VERACIOUS (he *is* the truth)
- TRANSCENDENT (he exists outside of the universe)
- IMMANENT (he exists within the universe)
- Ineffable / incomprehensible (we cannot fully explain him or know him)
- Unified / simple (there is only one God; he forms a complete whole)

Philosophers point out that some of these attributes are paradoxical, inconsistent with each other, or that they raise some worrying questions about the nature of the universe and humans' place within it. These problems are shown in the table on p32 and are discussed in the following pages.

Some of the inconsistencies between God's attributes and/or the universe can be used as arguments which aim to prove that God does not exist. Such arguments maintain that a being with such an incoherent nature cannot exist, therefore either God has different attributes from the ones we usually ascribe to him (so he is not very close to our idea of God), or he doesn't exist at all.

Is God like humans?

Philosophers sometimes distinguish between COMMUNICABLE ATTRIBUTES of God (attributes which human beings can also have, such as goodness) and INCOMMUNICABLE ATTRIBUTES of God (attributes which belong to God alone, such as transcendence and omnipotence).

How do we know God's attributes?

There are two approaches to theology:

- NATURAL THEOLOGY: using thought, reason, meditation etc. to understand God's attributes or his nature
- REVEALED THEOLOGY: using sacred texts (e.g. the Bible or Qur'an) where Gods or angels revealed themselves to people, and their experiences were recorded in the texts

Philosophers generally (but not always) prefer the natural theological approach. In this module – and more generally in Western philosophy – the God referred to probably closely resembles the JUDEO-CHRISTIAN God, or Allah, the Islamic God.

Omniscient	Eternal	Everlasting	Omni-benevolent	Immutable	Immanent	Transcendent	
Problem of evil (p46)	Problem of divine action (p33 and p40)	Problem of creation (p40)	Problem of evil (p46)	God cannot change (p33)		Problem of divine action (p33)	Omnipotent
	Problem of free will (p36)	Knowing the future (p36)	Problem of evil (p46)	Changing knowledge (p35)	God knows evil (p35)	What does God know? (p34)	Omniscient
Problem of evil (p46)	Problem of divine action (p38)			Old / New Testament (p38)	God is evil (p39)	Problem of divine action (p38)	Omni-benevolent
					Space-time incoherence (p40)		Eternal
						Space-time incoherence (p40)	Everlasting

This table shows some of the most important inconsistencies between God's attributes. Some attributes also have problems in themselves – such as omnibenevolence (Euthyphro dilemma, p43) or omnipotence (paradox of the stone, p41). Some attributes are only problematic when combined with other attributes, such as omnipotence, omnibenevolence and omniscience (problem of evil, p46).

Omnipotence

Overview

Key philosopher: Aquinas

Omnipotence means being all-powerful and able to do anything. Philosophers disagree on whether this means God is able to do *anything*, or just LOGICALLY POSSIBLE things.

Aquinas suggests that God can only do what is logically possible. He can't change the past; he can't change the laws of mathematics so that 2 + 2 = 5; he can't do something contradictory such as making an item both exist and not exist at the same time; he can't sin by creating something evil; he can't lessen his powers or make himself not exist.

So Aquinas and others claim that God can do anything logically possible which doesn't alter his power or his fundamental nature. However, critics point out that this doesn't sound like true omnipotence, but more like DEATH BY A THOUSAND QUALIFICATIONS.

Paradox of the stone

The omnipotence of God is problematic in itself: if God can do anything, then he should be able to create an enormous stone – one so big that God himself cannot move it. Whether God can't create the stone or he can't move the stone, there's something he can't do – therefore he is not omnipotent (see p41)

Problem of divine action

There is an inconsistency between God's omnipotence and the nature of his existence: if God exists outside of the universe (he's TRANSCENDENT) or outside of time (he's ETERNAL) then how can he perform actions within space and time? For example, how was it possible for God to create the universe or perform miracles – does his omnipotence enable him to act within space and time even though he is outside of time? This does not seem possible (also see p38).

God cannot change

There is an inconsistency between omnipotence and IMMUTABILITY: if God has the power to do anything, then he should have the power to change himself. This argument can be summarised as:

1. If God can change himself, he is not immutable
2. If God cannot change himself, he is not omnipotent

C. Therefore, God cannot be both omnipotent and immutable

The response to this can come from someone such as Aquinas, who suggests that God cannot alter his fundamental nature, so God is omnipotent but cannot change himself.

The problem of evil

There is an inconsistency between omnipotence, OMNISCIENCE, OMNIBENEVOLENCE, and the existence of EVIL in the world (see p46). The suggestion is that if God is good, he knows that evil occurs, and he has the power to stop it, then why doesn't he stop it?

Omniscience

Overview

Key philosophers: Kretzmann, Kenny

OMNISCIENCE is the attribute of being all-seeing or all-knowing. This would mean that God can see – or know – everything that is taking place in the universe at once (and presumably without effort).

However, there are problems with the attribute of omniscience.

Knowing the logically impossible

Some philosophers question whether omniscience must involve knowing what it is LOGICALLY IMPOSSIBLE or nonsensical to know. For example, does God know the volume of a triangular ball? However, most philosophers agree that God cannot know logical impossibilities such as this.

What does God know?

Philosophers distinguish different types of knowledge:

- ACQUAINTANCE KNOWLEDGE – knowing a person or place, or knowing attributes about them, such as "I know Peter"
- ABILITY KNOWLEDGE – knowing how to do something, such as dancing or driving a car
- PROPOSITIONAL KNOWLEDGE – knowing facts such as "London is the capital city of the UK" or "Tigers are big cats"

If God is INCORPOREAL (non-physical) and TRANSCENDENT (outside of the universe) then it seems nonsense to claim that God knows how to swim breaststroke, bake a cake, plaster a wall (etc); it does not seem possible for God to have any of the ability knowledge which humans or animals possess.

Theologians may respond by suggesting that God does not have ability knowledge, but he possesses all the propositional knowledge about the activity – for example, he knows the physics of swimming (forces, buoyancy, density and so on). Nonetheless, there is a difference between having propositional knowledge about something, and knowing how to do it yourself, or knowing what the experience is like (see Mary's black and white room, p116). So if God doesn't know *how* to swim or what it is *like* to swim, then there is something he doesn't know, so he's not omniscient.

God knows evil

If theologians insist that God does know what it is like to swim, dance (etc) whether because he is IMMANENT or OMNIPRESENT, or because he knows all propositional knowledge, then the theologians must also admit that God knows what it is like to do something evil. God knows all the propositional knowledge about the Holocaust, child tortures, school shootings etc, and if propositional knowledge allows God to have ability or acquaintance knowledge, then they must admit that God knows what it is like to murder, rape, torture, abuse children, and so on.

Clearly this conflicts with his OMNIBENEVOLENCE, and so the easiest solution for the theologian is to admit that God doesn't know what it is like to torture, rape etc – and so he is not truly omniscient.

Changing knowledge

There is an inconsistency between omniscience and IMMUTABILITY (particularly if God is also IMMANENT and/or EVERLASTING). Kretzmann gives an argument which can be summarised as:

1. God is (supposedly) immutable – he doesn't change
2. God is (supposedly) omniscient – he knows everything
3. As events in the universe occur, the universe changes, so God's knowledge of them changes
4. If God's knowledge changes, God has changed
5. If God has changed he is not immutable

C. Therefore, God cannot be both omniscient and immutable

Kretzmann attempts to refine premise 2 so that God doesn't need to know everything – only everything which it is LOGICALLY POSSIBLE for him to know and which doesn't limit his knowledge. However he dismisses this refinement as unsuccessful as the problem still remains: it is logically possible for God to know the future, and so the inconsistency remains. Kretzmann suggests this proves that an omniscient and immutable being can't exist.

Knowing the future

The above problem can be stated solely as an inconsistency between God's omniscience and his being EVERLASTING (without reference to immutability). If God exists within time, then he does not know what is about to happen in the future; this would mean that God is not omniscient. This can be summarised as:

1. If God exists within time, then he does not know the future
2. If God does not know the future then he is not omniscient

C. Therefore, God cannot be both everlasting and omniscient

One possible response to this (and to the inconsistency between immutability and omniscience), is to suggest that God (always) knows everything that will happen throughout time because he is eternal. However, this raises problems for free will (see below).

The problem of free will

There is an inconsistency between God's omniscience, his being ETERNAL, and the existence of human free will. The problem is that if God is omniscient then he knows the future, but if he knows the future, then human free will is an illusion, and we are not free to do as we please. The argument can be summarised as:

1. God is omniscient – he knows everything
2. Everything includes my future choices
3. If God knows my future choices before I've made them, then my choices are predetermined

C. Therefore, either God isn't omniscient, or humans have no free will

The problem of free will cannot be satisfactorily solved by conceding that we have no free will; we believe humans have free will, and we see it as valuable. But more importantly, it is an essential factor in God's judgement of us: how can we be judged as good or evil if our actions weren't under our control? It wouldn't be fair to send someone to Hell for an action which was out of his control, and so if God is OMNIBENEVOLENT (or at the very least, fair) then free will needs to be guaranteed.

Kenny phrased the problem of free will as two mutually incompatible statements: one of these statements must be denied if we are to solve the problem of free will – but denying either option is unappealing.

- God's omniscience means that he knows beforehand everything that people will do
- Some actions of people are free

Possible solutions

Aquinas suggests that God knows what will happen, but we still have free will. However this is unconvincing and merely restates the problem as if it is a solution.

Another option is to suggest that God is everlasting rather than eternal, however this is also problematic – see p36.

Another possible solution is to say that God only knows things which aren't a result of free will. However this is unconvincing because almost all events (on Earth, at least) are a result of free will. This would mean that God's knowledge is so limited that he'd know almost nothing about what was going to happen on Earth; this doesn't sound like omniscience.

The problem of evil

There is an inconsistency between omniscience, OMNIPOTENCE, OMNIBENEVOLENCE, and the existence of EVIL in the world (see p46). The suggestion is that if God is good, he knows evil occurs, and he has the power to stop it, then why doesn't he stop it?

Omnibenevolence

Overview

Omnibenevolence means being all-good or all-loving; it is sometimes just referred to as benevolence.

Aquinas, Aristotle and Plato conceive of omnibenevolence as a type of perfection, encompassing all his other qualities such as omniscience, omnipotence, and so on. It's not that God is good *in addition to* these other perfections; rather, his other perfections interconnect to form his ultimate perfection – his supreme goodness.

Other philosophers such as Augustine concentrate on omnibenevolence as a source of moral guidance: God is the very definition of goodness. We can also view omnibenevolence as a feature of God's character and the way he treats humans.

Old and new testament

There is an inconsistency between omnibenevolence and IMMUTABILITY (for the Christian God, at least). In the Old Testament of the Bible, God does not seem omnibenevolent; rather, he seems vengeful, devious and punitive. In the New Testament, he seems more benevolent – but it is not clear whether God has changed, or whether he still retains his vengeful traits which he displayed in the Old Testament. Either way, this is problematic, and the argument can be summarised as:

1. God in the Old Testament seems vengeful
2. God in the New Testament seems omnibenevolent
3. If God has changed (from the Old Testament to the New Testament) then he is not immutable
4. If God has not changed, then he is still vengeful and therefore not omnibenevolent

C. Therefore, either God is not immutable, or God is not omnibenevolent

Some responses to this problem suggest that the Old Testament does not depict the one true God, or that the Old Testament is metaphorical, sketchy, or not to be trusted. Other responses suggest that God *is* indeed vengeful, but this is out of his love for humans. This theme is explored in some of the theodicies on p49.

Problem of divine action

There is an inconsistency between God's omnibenevolence and his being TRANSCENDENT and/or ETERNAL. It is suggested that God's omnibenevolence is demonstrated in his actions towards humans, such as sparing people's lives, answering prayers and performing miracles. But if he is outside of the universe and outside of time, it seems impossible for him to perform acts within space and time (also see p33).

Euthyphro dilemma

There is a problem with the concept of omnibenevolence as a source of moral guidance: does God command an act because it is good, or is the act good because God commands it? This is the Euthyphro dilemma (see p43).

The problem of evil

There is an inconsistency between omniscience, OMNIPOTENCE, OMNIBENEVOLENCE, and the existence of EVIL in the world (see p46). The suggestion is that if God is good, he knows evil occurs, and he has the power to stop it, then why doesn't he stop it?

God is evil?

If God exists throughout the universe, and the universe contains evil, then it seems God is at least partially evil. This is sometimes phrased as though it is an inconsistency between omnibenevolence and IMMANENCE, but it is more accurately expressed as an inconsistency between omniscience and OMNIPRESENCE – the notion that God exists everywhere in the universe.

PANTHEISTS such as Spinoza believe that God is within and throughout the universe: God *is* the universe. Given that evil things occur in the universe then this leads us to the undesirable conclusion that God does not just allow evil – God is (at least partly) evil. Pantheism is rejected by most religious doctrines for this and other reasons.

Eternal or Everlasting

Overview

It is said that God has always existed and will always exist, but how this manifests itself is a source of disagreement among philosophers and theologians. In everyday language, we use words like eternal, timeless and everlasting to mean the same thing, but they have different meanings in the Metaphysics of God:

- *Eternal*: exists outside of time
- *Everlasting*: exists within time, but has always and will always exist

The word 'timeless' is often taken to be synonymous with eternal, but the terms eternal and everlasting are more precise.

God may be eternal or he may be everlasting, but he cannot be both (and no one claims that he is both).

The Bible mostly implies that God is eternal (he created the universe, so must exist outside of space-time), yet some passages suggest that God may exist within time (as everlasting).

Space-time incoherence

Science tells us that space and time are fused as a single continuum; in other words, they are interlinked. This means that God's TRANSCENDENCE is only coherent with his being eternal – because if he is outside of space he must also be outside of time. Similarly, God's IMMANENCE is only coherent with his being everlasting – because if he is within space he must also be within time.

- Transcendence is inconsistent with being everlasting (God cannot be outside of space but inside of time)
- Immanence is inconsistent with being eternal (God cannot be inside of space but outside of time)

Problem of divine action

There is an inconsistency between God being eternal, his OMNIPOTENCE, and his interactions with us. If God exists outside of time, it is implausible that he performs acts within time, such as creating the world, miracles, and answering our prayers.

If we maintain that God cannot perform acts within space-time, then he does not seem omnipotent, and it seems incompatible with a personal God who intervenes in our lives to help us out.

Problem of creation

There is an inconsistency between God being everlasting and his OMNIPOTENCE. This comes about because if God exists within time, then he did not create time, and therefore he is not omnipotent.

Problem of free will

Whether God is ETERNAL or EVERLASTING, there is an inconsistency between his omniscience and the existence of human free will. If God exists in time then he cannot know the future, and so he is not omniscient, but if he does know the future then we have no free will (see p36).

This argument can be summarised as:

1. If God is everlasting (within time) then he cannot know the future
2. If God doesn't know the future then he is not omniscient
3. If God is eternal (outside of time) and omniscient then he knows the future
4. If God knows the future then human free will is an illusion

C. Therefore, God's omniscience is incompatible with human free will

Paradox of the Stone

Overview

Key philosophers: Averroes, Mavrodes, Savage

The paradox of the stone is a problem for the OMNIPOTENCE of God. It can be used as an argument against the existence of an omnipotent being. The paradox of the stone involves asking whether God can create a stone so heavy that he cannot lift / move it.

The question was first posed by Averroes, also known as Ibn Rushd. It can be summarised as:

Can God make a stone so heavy that he cannot move it?

1. If God can't make the stone, then he's not omnipotent
2. If God makes the stone but can't move it, then he's not omnipotent

C. Therefore, God is not omnipotent

The argument is intended to show that omnipotence is a nonsensical attribute for a being to have, and so if God does exist he is not omnipotent (although he would fail to be a God on many definitions if he lacked omnipotence) or more seriously, no God at all exists.

Mavrodes' version

Mavrodes argues that the paradox doesn't disprove God's omnipotence, because asking God to create a stone he cannot lift is a contradiction. There can *be* no stone that God cannot lift; logically, such a stone cannot exist.

So the paradox is asking God to do something contradictory, and God needn't perform contradictory feats in order to be omnipotent. Mavrodes concludes that the paradox of the stone poses no challenge to God's omnipotence. Mavrodes' argument can be summarised as:

1. An omnipotent being has the power to lift anything
2. It's contradictory to ask whether a being who can lift anything, can make a stone which he cannot lift
3. Being unable to perform something contradictory does not disprove omnipotence

C. Therefore, the paradox of the stone doesn't disprove God's omnipotence

Mavrodes' argument may seem convincing, but there is a strong response from Savage.

Response from Savage

Savage criticises Mavrodes because his argument misses the point: of course the paradox is contradictory – because it's a paradox! Savage points out that the paradox of the stone is not designed to prove that God isn't omnipotent, but that an omnipotent being itself is logically impossible.

Savage offers a line of reasoning without any reference to God, which he calls Version B:

Either: (i) X can create a stone which X cannot lift
or (ii) X cannot create a stone which X cannot lift

Whether (i) or (ii) is true, X cannot do something. If we then try to claim that X is omnipotent, we'll see the contradiction and conclude that the existence of an omnipotent being is impossible. Savage argues that it is this Version B which needs addressing.

Although Savage criticises Mavrodes' approach, and constructs Version B, Savage only does this to avoid ATTACKING A STRAW MAN. In other words, Savage creates Version B to present the paradox of the stone in its strongest form, then he challenges it.

Savage's argument challenging Version B can be summarised as:

1. Imagine two beings, X and Y: X makes stones, and Y lifts stones
2. If X and Y are omnipotent, whatever stone X creates, Y can lift it
3. X is not limited in his power, as he can create a stone of any size or weight
4. Y is not limited in his power, as he can lift a stone of any size or weight
5. X and Y can both be omnipotent without contradiction
6. X and Y can be the same person without contradiction

C. Therefore, a being (e.g. God) can be able to make any stone, and be able to lift any stone, without contradiction

Savage's argument seems fairly convincing, but premise 2 is the important one to challenge: if whatever stone X creates, Y can lift it, then X cannot create a stone that Y cannot lift. This means that although Y has the power to lift anything, X does not have the power to make anything (namely a stone that Y cannot lift). This means that X is not omnipotent, and the paradox of the stone remains.

Euthyphro Dilemma

Overview

Key philosophers: Plato, Socrates

The Euthyphro dilemma is a problem for the OMNIBENEVOLENCE of God. It was originally written by Plato as a dialogue between Socrates and a man called Euthyphro. They discuss what is meant by PIETY (goodness / holiness), and Socrates asks whether something is good because God commands it, or whether God commands it because it's good. In other words, is a good act only good because God says it's good, or would it still be good even without God saying so?

The two horns

There are two possible answers to the Euthyphro dilemma which Socrates considers; they are called the two horns. (Note that some texts refer to the horns the other way around, so be sure to explain which horn you are referring to in an exam response.)

First horn	Second horn
God's commands are what makes an action good. This is troublesome for morality as it means that morality is contingent upon God: God could command rape and murder and that would make them good.	A good action is already good, regardless of whether God commands it. This is troublesome for God as it means morality and goodness are independent from God: God is not a necessary part of morality.

First horn

The first horn is the suggestion that particular acts are good simply because they are commanded by God. This means that God defines goodness; it doesn't exist above and beyond him.

Problem with the first horn

God could command us to do anything, and it would become morally good. This could be a trivial act such as eating a banana – and we would be forced to say that this act is morally good, as it came from God.

God could even command us to commit vile, cruel acts which we generally consider to be immoral, such as rape, genocide, and torturing children. There are numerous examples in the Bible when God commands someone to do an act which we tend to think of as wrong. For example, in 1 Samuel 15:2-3, God commands Saul and the Israelites to commit genocide. If we are to believe the first horn, then we must conclude that it is a morally good act for Saul and the Israelites to commit genocide in this instance, since God commanded it.

Teleological suspension of the ethical

Kierkegaard argues that in instances where God commands something which seems immoral, it is still our duty to carry out such commands, and doing so is morally good. For example, when God commands Abraham to sacrifice his son Isaac, Abraham is right to (attempt to) do so. Kierkegaard maintains that whatever God commands is good, and faith in God should be placed above our ethical intuitions: he calls this the "teleological suspension of the ethical". However, this is an argument which many theists find distasteful.

God could, but wouldn't

An alternative response to the first horn is to maintain that God *could* command a cruel act – and that act would be morally good – but God *wouldn't* do this because of his OMNIBENEVOLENT nature.

Whilst this is a view which many theists ascribe to, it doesn't seem to adequately answer whether it was genuinely good for Saul to commit genocide and Abraham to (attempt to) murder his son.

Is God good?

If goodness or benevolence is defined by God, then saying "God is good" or "God is omnibenevolent" is no different from saying "God does the things which he defines as good" which seems rather meaningless.

Second horn

The second horn is the suggestion that goodness exists independently of God; God does not define goodness, he simply endorses the goodness that is already there. According to Plato in his account of the Forms, good things have an objective reality, and it is God's conformity to this goodness which makes God good.

Limit to God's power

If we wish to be moral, we do not need to appeal to God, since goodness exists beyond God. If morality exists independently of God, then God does not have the power to change or define moral laws – this suggests that he is not OMNIPOTENT. If the moral laws are unchangeable even by God, then the moral laws are supremely good, but God is not; he is only CONTINGENTLY good, rather than NECESSARILY good. Why should we worship God as a moral authority, when he is not the highest moral authority?

God is unnecessary

If the second horn is correct, then God plays little or no part in morality, since moral laws exist above and beyond God. If God ceased to exist, moral laws would still continue to exist. According to Ockham's razor, unnecessary parts of a theory can be dispensed with; this means that we can be moral simply by adhering to moral laws; God is not a necessary part of morality.

God is evil

If moral rules exist beyond God, and if these moral rules include tenets such as 'do not kill' and 'do not encourage others to kill' then God has broken these moral rules. For example, God causes natural disasters and plagues ('acts of God') (see p47) and God told Abraham to kill his son Isaac, and Saul to commit genocide. This casts doubt on God's OMNIBENEVOLENCE.

Furthermore, if God usually follows the moral rules but didn't on these occasions, then he is not IMMUTABLE.

Arguments Relating to the Existence of God

Overview

Arguments relating to the existence of God come in two forms:

- Arguments attempting to demonstrate the non-existence of God (or at least, that God's attributes are not those offered by theology)
- Arguments attempting to demonstrate the existence of God (with the attributes offered by theology)

No arguments have been universally accepted as proving or disproving the existence of a God as described by theology.

Arguments against the existence of God

- *The problem of evil* (why does a loving and all-powerful God permit evil in the world?) (see below)

The following can also be used as arguments against the existence of God, but are not classified as such by the specification (see p141)

- *The paradox of the stone* (can God create a stone too heavy for him to lift?) (p41)
- *The Euthyphro dilemma* (are acts good because God commands them, or does God command them because they are good?) (p43)
- *Problems with the incompatibility of God's attributes* (p32)

Arguments for the existence of God

- *Ontological arguments* (DEDUCTIVE A PRIORI arguments which use the definition of God to prove that God must exist) (p55)
- *Teleological (design) arguments* (things in the universe work so well that they must have been designed by God) (p62)
- *Cosmological arguments* (every event has a cause, and if we work backwards then the first cause of everything is God) (p68)

Each of these arguments has different versions, so avoid referring to (e.g.) "the ontological argument" as if it is a single entity. Instead, refer to one version in particular, such as "Anselm's ontological argument". If you wish to criticise all versions of a particular argument, then write "(all) ontological arguments".

Problem of Evil

Overview	**Key philosophers:** Epicurus, Mackie, Hume

The problem of evil is an argument against the existence of God. The suggestion is that an OMNIBENEVOLENT and OMNIPOTENT God would not allow evil in the world. Given that we know evil exists, this shows that God does not exist.

Types of evil

Within the Metaphysics of God, EVIL is taken to mean the pain and suffering of living beings (e.g. animals, humans). This suffering may be physical (pain, starvation, illness) or mental (fear, misery). Evil is typically split into moral evil and natural evil:

Moral evil	Natural (or physical) evil
The pain, misery and suffering caused by human actions, such as war, rape, genocide, murder, bullying, child abuse, burglary, and others.	The pain, misery and suffering which happens independently of human actions, such as natural disasters (earthquakes, tsunamis, volcano eruptions); health issues (illnesses, disabilities, and disorders).

Some of the attempted solutions to the problem of evil only address one type of evil; failing to address both types of evil is a weakness of any response. However, the distinction between moral and natural evil is not entirely clear-cut.

For example, some illnesses such as heart disease and cancer are often partially a result of people's lifestyle choices, and some 'natural' disasters such as floods are caused by climate change, which humans are responsible for.

Privation of the good

Augustine and Aquinas saw evil not as an entity in itself, but as an absence of goodness ("the privation of good"). This was developed from Plato and Aristotle's accounts of goodness, which was characterised by fulfilling a purpose. Any thing (whether a chair, a wasp, or a human) which fulfils its purpose can be called 'good'; if it doesn't fulfil its purpose, it is not good. If the purpose of a human is to be kind, peaceful and cooperative, then humans who kill and harm others are not fulfilling their purpose and are therefore not good – they are evil.

The inconsistent triad

An INCONSISTENT TRIAD comprises three propositions which cannot all be true without contradiction. In the problem of evil, the three propositions are often taken to be (see right):

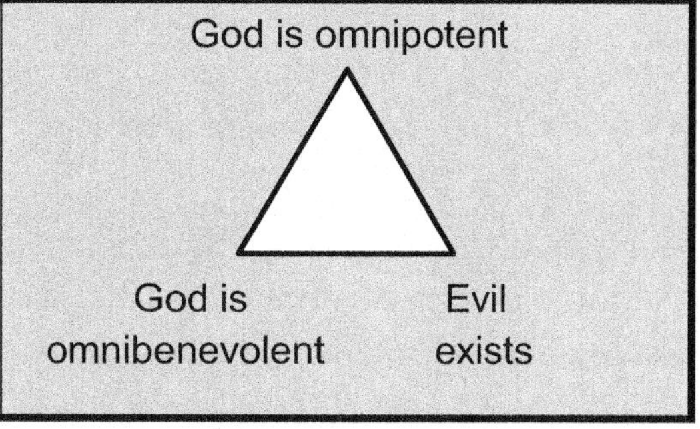

Although the inconsistent triad is succinct, it is an incomplete way of presenting the problem of evil, since it omits the proposition 'God is omniscient'. This is needed, or else a very simple solution to the inconsistent triad is to respond that God is unaware of all the evil that exists, and that's why he doesn't stop it.

Formulations

There are two formulations to the problem of evil:

- *The logical problem of evil:* this is a DEDUCTIVE, A PRIORI argument which aims to show that it's a logical contradiction to believe in a God who permits evil to exist.
- *The evidential problem of evil:* this is an INDUCTIVE, A POSTERIORI argument which presents evidence to show that the existence of evil makes it less likely that God exists.

Logical problem of evil

Epicurus was one of the first philosophers to outline the logical problem of evil. His deductive argument can be summarised as:

1. Evil exists
2. If God is willing but unable to remove evils, then he is feeble, which is not a characteristic of God
3. If God is able but unwilling to remove evils, then he is wicked, which is not a characteristic of God
4. If God is neither willing nor able to remove evils, then he is feeble *and* wicked, which are not characteristics of God
5. (implied) God cannot be both willing and able to remove evils, because they still exist

C. Therefore, God does not exist

Mackie outlines the logical problem of evil as:

1. God is (supposedly) omnipotent
2. God is (supposedly) wholly good
3. Evil exists
4. A good being eliminates evil as much as it can
5. There are no limits to what an omnipotent being can do

C. Therefore, God does not exist

As a deductive argument, the logical problem of evil is intended to show that it is a contradiction for an omnibenevolent, omnipotent God to exist alongside evil, or to have created a world with evil in it. If we accept Epicurus' or Mackie's arguments as sound, then they have proven without doubt that God does not exist.

Evidential problem of evil

This inductive (or abductive) argument is put forward by Hume and others. It does not aim to show that theists hold *contradictory* beliefs; only to show that given all the evil in the world, the existence of God seems unlikely. The argument can be summarised as:

1. There exists a great deal of evil in the world
2. There are two possibilities:
   (a) There exists an omnipotent, omniscient, omnibenevolent God who created our world
   (b) There is no such God
3. Hypothesis (b) seems far more likely than hypothesis (a)

C. Therefore, God does not exist

Responses to the Problem of Evil

Overview	**Key philosophers:** Plantinga, Hick

The problem of evil states that an omnipotent, omnibenevolent God would not allow evil to exist (see p46). Responses to the problem of evil fall into four main categories:

1. **Limited God / alternative theologies**: God exists but is not omnipotent, omniscient, and omnibenevolent (he lacks at least one of these features).	2. **Afterlife defence**: God exists, and is omnibenevolent, omnipotent and omniscient; the evils of this world are balanced by greater good in the afterlife.
3. **Free will defence**: God exists, and is omnibenevolent, omnipotent and omniscient, and the evils of this world are the consequence of a greater good – free will.	4. **Soul making defence**: God exists, and is and is omnibenevolent, omnipotent and omniscient, and the evils of this world lead to a greater good – humans fulfilling their potential.

Responses and theodicies

A THEODICY is an attempt to explain or justify God's actions, for example to explain why he allows evil to persist. All of the above list are genuine responses to the problem of evil, but response 1 is not a theodicy. Responses 2, 3, and 4 can be theodicies, depending on their formulation.

Atheists' reaction

ATHEISTS react to the problem of evil by stating that no God exists: moral and natural evils occur because God is not around to stop them from occurring. However, this is not considered a genuine *response* to the problem of evil, as it merely agrees that the problem of evil demonstrates God does not exist.

Sartre argues that there is no God, and this leads people to a feeling of abandonment as they confront the meaninglessness of existence. We must endure pain and suffering which often occur without reason or explanation. People who cause moral evil may never have to answer for their crimes, as there is no external source of morality or redemption.

Strength	Criticisms
• Adequately explains the existence of both moral and natural evils.	• Not a genuine response to the problem of evil. • Not a response favoured by theists.

Alternative theologies

One way to respond to the problem of evil is to maintain that God exists but that he is not omnipotent, omniscient, and/or omnibenevolent. This is called offering an ALTERNATIVE THEOLOGY, because the God which is referred to is not the God typically depicted in SACRED TEXTS.

For example, an alternative theology might suggest one or more of the following:

God exists but he is not omnipotent, so he can't stop (all) evil from occurring.	God exists, but he is not omniscient, so he doesn't know about (all) the evil which occurs.	God exists, but he is not omnibenevolent, so he allows some evil to occur, or even causes some evil himself.

A variant of the denial of God's omnipotence is the suggestion that God exists and is exceptionally powerful, but one or more evil Gods also exist, which makes it impossible for God to fully eradicate evil. This is a form of PROCESS THEOLOGY.

Strengths	Criticisms
• Adequately explains how evil and a God-like being can co-exist. • The idea of a finitely powerful, good and knowledgeable being can be compatible with some religions and even with atheism.	• A being which is not omnipotent, omniscient or omnibenevolent is perhaps not a God. • Not a response favoured by many theists.

Afterlife defence

The AFTERLIFE DEFENCE is a theodicy which suggests that our suffering on Earth pales into insignificance when compared with the eternal bliss of the afterlife. Any amount of suffering during a lifetime is infinitesimal when compared with eternity in Heaven. (Also, those who inflict suffering in this life will be punished with eternal damnation in Hell.)

Strength

- This is a response favoured by many theists.

Criticisms

- The afterlife defence merely states that our suffering is outweighed by eternal bliss, but doesn't really *explain* why God allows our suffering; eternal bliss *and* a nice life on Earth would be better than eternal bliss and suffering on Earth.

Criticisms

- The idea of Heaven raises many questions such as whether it exists outside of space-time, whether someone can move from Hell to Heaven if they repent, how acts are weighed up by God, and so on.
- The idea of Hell is an even greater 'evil' than the ones on Earth, so it's hard to reconcile an omnibenevolent God with the idea of souls burning in Hell for eternity.

Free will defence

The free will defence rests on the idea that humans have free will, and so sometimes evil occurs because humans choose to do evil things – but a life with free will *and* evil is better than a life without free will *or* evil.

The free will defence can be formulated as a theodicy, such as that by Augustine: he suggests that moral and natural evil occur because of 'original sin' – namely, the fall of Lucifer, and Eve eating from the Tree of Knowledge in the Garden of Eden.

Plantinga puts forward a free will defence, but it is not a theodicy, as it does not *explain why* God permits evil; it just suggests that free will is *one possible reason* why God permits evil. It can be summarised as:

1. An omnipotent God can create any kind of world
2. A world with free will is better than a world without free will
3. Therefore, an omnipotent and omnibenevolent God will give beings free will
4. God cannot cause beings with free will to do what is morally correct
5. Beings with free will might choose to do what is morally wrong (evil)

C. Therefore, free beings (humans) are the source of evil in the world

Plantinga's free will defence challenges Mackie's premise 4 (see p48) that a good being eliminates evil as much as it can. Plantinga gives us reason to believe that a good being may not always eliminate evil – because human free will is more valuable than avoiding evil.

Criticism by Flew

Flew suggests that Plantinga commits the fallacy of the FALSE DILEMMA (see p16). Plantinga presents only two possible options, namely that either (a) God gives people free will (and evil occurs), or (b) All people are mindless automatons without any free will (and no evil occurs). However Flew suggests that God could have created a world (W*) where people have pleasant dispositions *and* free will. Flew argues that W* would have been better than our current world, so an omnibenevolent God should have created W*, rather than our world.

Response

It is questionable whether the people in W* genuinely have free will. In W*, God has manipulated people's personalities to prevent them from performing a wide range of acts (e.g. murder, rape, torture). It is an important part of theistic beliefs that humans have the free will to do *anything* so that God can judge their characters. If a person behaves morally because they have been manipulated into doing so, then they are not truly moral, and God would have very little to judge them on.

Criticism by Mackie

Mackie's criticism of Plantinga is similar to Flew's. His argument can be summarised as:

1. It's logically possible for an individual to choose to do good on any occasion
2. It's logically possible for an individual to choose to do good on *every* occasion throughout their life
3. If God is omnipotent, he can create any logically possible world

4. Therefore God could create a world in which everyone was genuinely free, but chose to do good on every occasion throughout their life
5. God did not create such a world

C. Therefore, an omnipotent, omnibenevolent God does not exist

Response by Plantinga

Plantinga responds that it's possible for there to be a person whose nature is so corrupt that whatever type of world God creates, the individual will always choose to commit at least one evil act. This is an unconvincing response because if God is *genuinely* omnipotent then he would ensure that such an individual did not exist.

Strengths of free will defence

- This is a response favoured by many theists.
- It adequately explains why moral evil occurs.

Criticisms of free will defence

- Perhaps a world without free will and without evil would be preferable to one with total freedom and uncontrollable evil.

Criticisms of free will defence

- Plantinga's free will defence only explains moral evil – it does not account for natural evils such as earthquakes and floods which kill people.
- Mackie's and Flew's criticisms of are quite convincing: it does seem possible to have free will and no (or very little) evil.

Soul-making defence

The soul-making defence suggests that the existence of evil leads to a greater good – humans growing as people and fulfilling their potential. This is because pain and suffering strengthen our souls.

Leibniz suggests that because God is omnibenevolent, he would choose to create the best possible universe. This means that the evil in our universe must serve some vital function, or God would have created a universe without evil in it. So from this we can conclude that the existence of evil must (in some way) help to make the universe the best possible universe it can be.

Hick's theodicy

Hick's theodicy is based on the work of St Irenaeus, and is known as the Irenaean theodicy. Unlike the free will defence, Hick does not see free will as an end in itself, but as a means to the end of improving human nature. He suggests that our suffering on Earth allows us to perfect our moral and spiritual nature, and achieve perfection in the afterlife.

According to Hick, God created an imperfect world with evil in it, so that we can work towards perfection. Hick refers to our (evil-ridden) world as the "VALE OF SOUL-MAKING", i.e. a place where we develop our souls, ready for Heaven.

Hick claims that *all* humans will eventually go to Heaven, although some (evil) people will need additional work on their souls in the afterlife, before they can ascend to Heaven.

Hick suggests that God doesn't make it obvious to us that he exists, nor that Heaven awaits us, because that would cause us to act morally out of fear and selfishness, rather than genuine goodness. Instead, God maintains the mystery through EPISTEMIC DISTANCE.

Strengths of soul-making defence

- This is a response favoured by many theists.
- It explains the existence of both moral and natural evil.
- Eternal bliss in Heaven outweighs the suffering we undergo on Earth.

Criticisms of soul-making defence

- If pain and suffering help us develop, then people who torture and abuse others are actually doing *good* deeds by helping others develop; if suffering helps us, then why is *causing* suffering seen as evil?
- Suffering in the world seems arbitrary: some innocent children suffer immeasurably. It is uncomfortable to conclude that their suffering is in fact good for them as it's strengthening their souls.
- Some people hardly suffer at all in their lives, either because they live happily, or because they die very young: how are they to improve their souls? It seems they are losing out, according to Hick.

Burden of Proof

Overview | **Key philosopher:** Russell

The burden of proof refers to whose task it is to prove or disprove a particular claim: proving something is not always easy, so people typically want their opponents to have the burden of proof. Often, atheists suggest that the burden of proof lies with theists – that it's up to believers in God to prove God exists. Atheists suggest that if no one can prove God exists, then we should assume that God doesn't exist. Theists say the burden of proof lies with the atheists: unless they can prove God *doesn't* exist, then we should assume that God *does* exist.

Russell's teapot

Russell argues that the burden of proof lies with those claiming that God exists: theists should have to prove that God *does* exist; it is not up to atheists to prove God *doesn't* exist. He puts forward this analogy:

> If I suggested that between the Earth and Mars there is a china teapot orbiting the sun, nobody would be able to disprove my assertion because the teapot would be too small to be seen by even our most powerful telescopes. But if I then claimed that, since it cannot be disproved, we should accept it as true, people would think I was talking nonsense.

By this Russell means that when people make a claim that X exists, the burden of proof lies with the person making that claim; it is not the task of others to prove that X *doesn't* exist. We take this standpoint when people claim the existence of Bigfoot, aliens, the Loch Ness Monster, and so on; it is not our job to prove these things *don't* exist – it is their job to prove these things *do* exist.

Ontological Arguments

Overview | **Key philosophers:** Hume, Kant, Russell

Ontological arguments are DEDUCTIVE ARGUMENTS, meaning that if we accept the premises, and the logic is VALID, then we will have to accept the conclusion as certain. There are different versions of ontological arguments, so avoid writing "the ontological argument"; instead, refer to "(all) ontological arguments", or to one ontological argument in particular e.g. "Anselm's ontological argument".

Ontological arguments rest on the definition of God as perfect: the suggestion is that we can know that God exists A PRIORI because existence is part of God's definition. If an ontological argument succeeds then it would be a great achievement for humanity, as we'd be able to establish God's existence with certainty, and without the need for any experience.

Ontological arguments claim that "God exists" is ANALYTICALLY TRUE, in the same way as "brothers are male" and "triangles have 3 sides" are analytically true. Ontological arguments suggest that once you truly understand the meaning of the word 'God', you cannot help but agree that God exists.

Evaluation

The following strengths and criticisms can apply to all three of the ontological arguments (by Anselm, Descartes, and Malcolm).

Existential statements are synthetic

As an EMPIRICIST, Hume argues that nothing can have its existence proven A PRIORI. He argues that anything can be conceived of as existing or not existing, without contradiction. Ontological arguments try to prove God's existence by suggesting that it's ANALYTICALLY TRUE that God exists. Hume argues that "all existential statements are SYNTHETIC": by this he means that in order to know what exists and what does not exist, we must examine the *world* – we cannot discover whether something exists by examining the meanings of the words. Hume's argument can be summarised as:

1. Something can only be proven *a priori* if the opposite implies a contradiction
2. Nothing that is conceivable implies a contradiction
3. Whatever can be conceived of as existent, can also be conceived of as non-existent
4. There is no being whose non-existence implies a contradiction

C. Therefore, there is no being whose existence can be proven *a priori*

Strength	Criticism
• Ontological arguments are (usually) DEDUCTIVELY VALID, so if the premises are true, it is a SOUND argument, and God's existence will be proven *a priori.*	• It does not seem possible to prove the existence of God simply by examining our idea of God, because our idea may be fictitious.

Criticisms

- Kant and Russell argue that saying something exists isn't a property / predicate of that thing; if I say "my car..." then I am implying that my car exists. If I finish the sentence with "...is blue" then I have given you more information (properties) about my car, but if I finish with "...exists" then I've not given any additional information (properties) about my car.
- Schopenhauer calls ontological arguments a 'conjuring trick', because the conclusion is concealed within the premises, only to be revealed at the end, as if by surprise. In other words, ontological arguments BEG THE QUESTION because they assume the very thing they are trying to prove (a perfect God exists).
- Even theists are frequently unconvinced by ontological arguments!

Remember that even if all ontological arguments fail to prove that God exists, this does not mean that God definitely *doesn't* exist – only that it hasn't been *proven*.

Anselm's Ontological Argument

Overview

Key philosophers: Anselm, Gaunilo

Anselm's ontological argument is based on the idea that it is greater to exist than not to exist. His argument can be summarised as:

1. God is the greatest being ("that than which nothing greater can be conceived")
2. God exists as an idea in the mind
3. It is greater to exist in reality *and* the mind, rather than only in the mind
4. If God only existed in the mind, then we could conceive of a greater being (i.e. one which existed in reality)
5. There can be nothing greater than God

C. Therefore, God must exist (both in reality and in the mind)

Anselm notes that an ATHEIST (whom he refers to as a 'fool') can conceive of a greatest possible being (God) but denies that such a being exists. Anselm suggests that this is a contradiction because an existent God is greater than a non-existent God, so a non-existent 'God' isn't the greatest possible being.

Gaunilo's criticism

Gaunilo puts forward a criticism of Anselm's argument: he suggests that anything can be defined into existence using Anselm's argument. Gaunilo constructs the following COUNTER-EXAMPLE to highlight the absurdity of Anselm's reasoning:

1. One can imagine an island greater than which nothing can be conceived (the most perfect island conceivable, greater than all other lands)
2. The perfect island exists as an idea in the mind
3. It is greater to exist in reality as well as in the mind, rather than only in the mind
4. If the perfect island existed only in the mind, then we could conceive of a greater island (i.e. one which existed in reality)
5. There can be no island greater than the perfect island

C. Therefore, this perfect island must exist (both in reality and in the mind)

Gaunilo's argument follows the same LOGICAL FORM as Anselm's argument, to demonstrate that simply conceiving of a perfect X does not prove that the perfect X exists. This form of argument could define anything into existence: the perfect man, the perfect unicorn, the perfect spaceship. Since we can deny that the perfect island exists, Gaunilo's argument shows that we can also deny that a perfect being (God) exists.

Response to Gaunilo

Islands and other things such as men, unicorns, spaceships and so on are not perfect by definition; God is perfect by definition. Islands are CONTINGENT and can be affected by other things whereas God is a NECESSARY BEING; he could not have been any different, as he is perfect by definition. Thus we can conceive of the perfect island not existing, because islands don't have perfection as part of their definition, whereas God does.

Strengths

- We often view an existent thing as greater than a non-existent thing (a million pounds in reality would be better than an imaginary million pounds).
- God does seem to have perfection as part of his definition: a God which was imperfect does not fit with our idea of God.

Criticisms

- Anselm's first premise is that God is the greatest being by definition, but this is an unjustified assertion – the definition has been made up by theists to support their belief, and has not been proven.
- Anselm's third premise (that it is greater to exist in reality than only the mind) is an unjustified opinion. It might be that actually, non-existence is greater than (or incomparable to) existence.
- Aquinas suggests that God is INEFFABLE and incomprehensible, meaning that we cannot know what it means to be the 'greatest possible being'.
- What can be conceived of is not a good guide to what exists; we can conceive of a spaceship travelling at a billion metres per second, yet science tells us that this is impossible. The existence of God would not rest on what humans can or cannot conceive of.

Also see the strengths and criticisms relating to all ontological arguments (p56).

Descartes' Ontological Argument

Overview | **Key philosopher:** Descartes

Descartes attempts GLOBAL SCEPTICISM in order to build up his knowledge from scratch, based only on INDUBITABLE truths. The idea of a triangle cannot be separated from the idea of a three-sided shape (because a triangle is three-sided by definition). Similarly, Descartes' idea of God cannot be separated from the idea of a supremely perfect being, (because God is supremely perfect by definition).

His ontological argument can be summarised as:

1. God is supremely perfect: he possesses all perfections
2. Existence is a perfection

C. Therefore, God must exist

Descartes sees existence as a perfection in the same way that omniscience and omnipotence are perfections. Descartes suggests that it would be a contradiction to think of a supremely perfect being as lacking a perfection such as existence, therefore God must exist.

Strength

- Descartes' ontological argument is deductively valid.

Criticisms

- Descartes suggests that a non-existent God is a contradiction, but it does not seem to be: most theists believe in their own God, but they conceive of other Gods as non-existent (e.g. a Christian conceives of the Roman Gods as non-existent). If it's possible to conceive of at least one God as non-existent, it's possible to conceive of *all* Gods as non-existent.

Criticisms

- Kant argues that existence is not a PREDICATE (property) of something. Instead, existence is a special kind of attribute which a thing needs in order to have any properties at all. Predicates describe features of objects or people, but existence does not describe any feature at all.
- Kant argues that even if we agree that '*if* God exists, he has the property of perfection', that does not prove that God *does* indeed exist.

Also see the strengths and criticisms relating to all ontological arguments (p56).

Malcolm's Ontological Argument

Overview

Key philosopher: Malcolm

Malcolm's ontological argument is derived from the idea that God is a being whose existence is NECESSARY rather than CONTINGENT. His argument can be summarised as:

1. One of the following scenarios must be the case:
   - Scenario 1: "God exists" is NECESSARILY FALSE: it is logically impossible for God to exist
   - Scenario 2: "God exists" is CONTINGENTLY FALSE: it was possible for him to exist, but it turns out that he doesn't exist
   - Scenario 3: "God exists" is CONTINGENTLY TRUE: it was possible for him not to exist, but it turns out that he does exist
   - Scenario 4: "God exists" is NECESSARILY TRUE: it is logically impossible for God not to exist
2. God is the greatest possible being, and nothing can affect his existence, so he cannot be contingent (Scenarios 2 and 3 are not possible)

3. Scenario 1 cannot be the case, as it is logically possible for God to exist
C. Therefore, "God exists" is necessarily true (God necessarily exists)

Malcolm's argument relies on the notion that contingency cannot be a feature of God – God doesn't depend on anything else for his existence, and nothing can affect his existence. This leaves the two possibilities that either it is logically impossible for God to exist, or that it's logically impossible for him *not* to exist. Since we can conceive of God existing, we can rule out scenario 1, and conclude that God necessarily exists.

Strength

- Most theists agree that God is a necessary being rather than a contingent one.

Criticisms

- God's definition as the greatest possible being is something which has been constructed by people; similarly, 'unicorns necessarily have horns' has been constructed by people, but this does not prove that unicorns exist or have horns.
- Kant argues that even if existence were a necessary property of God, that does not prove that God exists – it just shows that *if* God exists, he exists necessarily, not contingently.
- Premise 3 is unjustified: it seems possible to conceive of a God as existing or as not existing – we can conceive of Roman and Greek Gods as non-existent Gods.

Criticisms

- Malcolm may be presenting a FALSE DILEMMA: not all propositions fall neatly into one of his four possibilities. If an omniscient, omnipotent and long-lived (but not EVERLASTING) being exists, it's not clear whether "God exists" is true or false. Some people would agree that the being is God, while others would say God must be eternal or everlasting.
- Malcolm's assertion that God cannot be contingent is unjustified; if an omnipotent, omniscient, omnibenevolent being exists but that being happened to be contingent, we would probably still agree that it was God. Moreover, if we met such a being, there would be no way to tell whether he existed contingently or necessarily.

Also see the strengths and criticisms relating to all ontological arguments (p56).

Teleological (Design) Arguments

Overview

Key philosopher: Hume

Teleological arguments are described as INDUCTIVE ARGUMENTS (they make general observations which provide evidence for the conclusion) or ABDUCTIVE ARGUMENTS (inferences to the best explanation). Either way, they attempt to establish the existence of God A POSTERIORI.

When discussing the *design* of the universe, avoid mentioning the *creation* of the universe; this would be mixing teleological arguments with COSMOLOGICAL ARGUMENTS.

There are different versions of teleological arguments, so avoid writing "the teleological argument"; instead, refer to "(all) teleological arguments", or to one teleological argument in particular e.g. "Paley's teleological argument".

Types of design argument

Teleological arguments are also known as arguments from design, as they suggest that the universe was designed by someone – and that someone is God. The word 'teleological' comes from the Greek *telos*, meaning purpose or goal; the suggestion is that things in the universe are the way they are because they were designed with a goal or purpose in mind.

ARGUMENTS FROM DESIGN QUA PURPOSE suggest that things in the universe have a SPATIAL ORDER (the human eye is perfect for seeing, and animals are well suited to their habitats). This spatial order suggests that they were designed for those particular purposes (by God).	ARGUMENTS FROM DESIGN QUA REGULARITY suggest that things in the universe have a TEMPORAL ORDER (laws of motion and cause and effect are always consistent). This temporal order suggests that the universe was designed in such a way (by God).

Arguments from analogy

Hume's and Paley's arguments are ARGUMENTS FROM ANALOGY, as they use an example (a watch or another human-designed product) which supposedly bears some similarity to the universe.

Then the philosophers apply what we know about watches or other products (i.e. that they were designed) to the universe. In essence, Paley and Hume argue that a watch (or other product) is like the universe; watches and other products are designed, therefore the universe is designed.

1. A is like B
2. X is true of A

C. Therefore, X is true of B

Arguments from analogy take the form shown in the panel (right); the assumption is that if two things are similar in some known ways, they will (probably) be similar in another (unobserved) way. Arguments from analogy can be strong or weak, depending on the similarity between the things which are being compared.

For example, if we know some facts about alligators, we can reasonably infer some facts about crocodiles, but we can't infer very much at all about trains. This is because alligators and crocodiles are quite similar, but alligators and trains are not. It is questionable whether watches and other human-designed products are similar enough to the universe for the analogies to work.

Hume's design argument

Hume presents a teleological argument from analogy, however it is important to note that Hume is *not* convinced by his argument – he merely presents it to avoid ATTACKING A STRAW MAN, when he criticises design arguments. His argument can be summarised as:

1. Human-designed products fit the means to the ends
2. Nature resembles human-designed products in that the means fit the ends
3. Similar effects have similar causes
4. The cause of a human-designed product is an intelligent mind which designed it

C. Therefore, the cause of nature (the universe) is an intelligent mind which designed it (the mind is far greater than human minds)

Hume's criticisms

Hume gives several criticisms of design arguments from analogy: these are given on p65 as responses to Paley, but they can also serve as criticisms of Hume's own design argument.

Remember that even if all teleological (design) arguments fail to prove that God exists, this does not mean that God definitely *doesn't* exist – only that it hasn't been *proven*.

Paley's Design Argument

Overview

Key philosophers: Paley, Hume

Paley's teleological (design) argument is known as the ARGUMENT FROM DESIGN QUA PURPOSE, because he focuses on purpose of things within the universe (sometimes referred to as SPATIAL ORDER). Paley anticipates (and answers) several criticisms against his argument; his responses help to strengthen his argument.

The watch on the hill

Paley's argument is told as a parable that can be summarised as:

Imagine walking across the hills, and finding a watch. Upon examining the watch, you notice that it has several parts which work together, and the parts are made from appropriate materials which suit their function. By working together in a complex way, the parts produce a well-regulated motion (of the hands moving). If any of the parts had been different, the watch would not have worked properly. Upon finding such a watch, one would be compelled to conclude that there must have existed a designer who understood and designed the watch for its purpose. All the evidence of design which exists in the watch also exists in nature, but to a greater degree.

From this parable, Paley argues that just as the watch has been designed by a watchmaker, so the universe and everything in it has been designed by a designer: God. Paley suggests that if a watch was found by someone who had never even heard of watches before, its complexity and the way it functions would be sufficient for the person to realise it had been designed. His argument can be summarised as:

1. A watch has particular features (complex parts which work together perfectly for a specific purpose)
2. A watch has these features because it has been designed that way by an intelligent creator – a watchmaker
3. Anything which has complex parts which work together for a specific purpose must also have been designed by an intelligent creator
4. The universe has complex parts which work together for a specific purpose (but far more amazing and complex than a watch)

C. Therefore, the universe must have been designed by an intelligent creator (but far more amazing than a watchmaker) i.e. God

Epicurean hypothesis

Paley (and Hume) both consider whether the universe may have formed itself into an ordered system as a result of random chance. This is called the EPICUREAN HYPOTHESIS after Epicurus, who suggests that if time is infinite, matter will at times form itself into ordered arrangements, and it just so happens that it's in a state of order at the moment. Hume suggests that since the Epicurean hypothesis is no better or worse than the theory of a designer, we should suspend judgement.

Paley dismisses the possibility that our universe could have come about by chance, because things are so well suited to their purpose (human eyes, animals in their habitats, and so on).

Strengths

- There are some things which do seem to fit their purpose so well that it can be hard to believe they were not designed that way – for example, the eye is perfectly made; if it were any different, it wouldn't work.
- God as the designer of the universe explains why everything fits its purpose, whereas science has not (yet) been able to explain why everything fits its purpose.
- The FINE TUNING ARGUMENT combines the design argument with a belief in evolutionary science. The suggestion is that God designed the universe to enable evolution, and now God monitors and adjusts evolution to encourage creatures to develop in particular ways.

Criticisms

- Kant points out that even if Paley could prove the universe has been designed, we can't infer that it was designed by God. The universe's designer could have been finite, lacking in power, evil, and could now be long dead.

Criticisms

- Hume suggests that if a watch was malfunctioning, we would infer a lazy or incompetent designer. There are problems of spatial disorder, mass extinctions and other evils which can be seen as problems with the universe, so perhaps we should infer a designer who is not omnipotent or omnibenevolent (see p46).
- Paley and Hume note that we have experience of watches and other machines being designed, but we have no experience of universes being designed; the universe is a unique case.

Response: Swinburne supports Paley's argument by suggesting that we do not need direct experience of universe-making in order to know it was designed; we can just observe the design and infer a designer.

- The arrangement of parts for a purpose does not prove the existence of a designer.

Criticisms

- Charles Darwin's theory of evolution adequately explains how animals fit their habitats and how the human eye evolved, without reference to a designer or God.
- Hume points out that watches and other artefacts are often designed by teams of people; the universe may have been designed by a group of beings.
- Hume argues that an analogy between a human-made object and the universe is very weak; human-made objects are *part of* the universe.
- Paley and Hume suggest that if a watch was found by someone who had never seen any machine before (e.g. a caveman) then he would not know it had been designed.

Response: Paley points out that we know that the Egyptian Pyramids and Stonehenge were designed simply by looking at them, even though we're not sure *how* or *why* they were designed.

Swinburne's Design Argument

Overview | **Key philosopher:** Swinburne

Swinburne's teleological argument is known as the ARGUMENT FROM DESIGN QUA REGULARITY, because he focuses on the temporal order and regularity of the universe.

Swinburne notes that Paley's design argument focuses on REGULARITIES OF CO-PRESENCE (physical wonders such as the human eye), whereas Swinburne's argument centres on REGULARITIES OF SUCCESSION (temporal wonders). He suggests that these regularities fall into two categories:

- HUMAN REGULARITIES OF SUCCESSION: when humans cause things to happen, such as hitting a tennis ball or smashing a window.
- NATURAL REGULARITIES OF SUCCESSION: things which happen without human intervention, e.g. the way gravity and laws of motion cause objects to move in predictable ways.

In his design argument, Swinburne explains human regularities of succession via human free will and power, and he suggests that the only way to explain natural regularities of succession is via a being which has free will and power as humans do (but in much greater quantities). Since the universe is so large and complex, Swinburne concludes that the being who controls and designs it must be extremely complex, powerful, and immaterial. His argument can be summarised as:

1. Regularities of succession occur naturally (without human action) and as a result of human action
2. Humans have free will, and the intelligence and power to bring about human regularities of succession
3. Natural regularities of succession cannot be explained by human action, nor by other natural laws
4. The universe is immense and complex

C. Natural regularities of succession across the universe can only be explained by an immense, complex, immaterial being with free will, intelligence and power

Swinburne limits the scope of his conclusion: he does not assert that the universe was designed by an omnipotent, omniscient, omnibenevolent and perfect God. (This allows him to avoid Kant's criticism discussed on page 65.)

Strengths	**Criticisms**
• Swinburne is right to point out that it is amazing that laws of gravity and motion are so regular throughout the universe. • The existence of God is a plausible explanation for the natural regularities of succession. • It would require an immense mind (if not omniscience) to design and regulate all the laws of cause and effect in the universe.	• Swinburne draws an analogy between humans and God, suggesting that humans cause some regularities of succession, and so something greater (God) must cause other regularities, but this analogy is weak; we have no evidence that the cause of natural regularities must be anything like a human. • Premise 3 can be challenged: the Big Bang can be the cause of natural regularities of succession.

Criticisms

- Mackie argues that a race of powerful (physical) alien beings could design and control natural regularities of succession.

Response: A race of physical beings could not have been present at the dawn of time: how could they have evolved? Aliens could not manipulate the laws of space-time whilst existing within space-time.

- Swinburne admits his argument doesn't prove that there exists a God who is omniscient, omnipotent, omnibenevolent, eternal or everlasting – so in many ways, it is not an argument for the existence of God.
- Even if science cannot currently explain all laws of motion, we are explaining more all the time and one day we may be able to explain the universe without reference to God. Ancient cultures created Gods to explain weather and earthquakes but now we know the science behind these events; the same may happen for the universe's natural laws.

Response: If the existence of God can (currently) explain regularities, but science cannot, we should favour design arguments until science can explain them.

- A being could have designed the universe and later died; it needn't have been designed by an eternal or everlasting being.

Cosmological Arguments

Overview

Key philosopher: Aristotle

Most cosmological arguments are INDUCTIVE ARGUMENTS which attempt to establish God's existence A POSTERIORI. They set out to explain what caused the universe to exist and they conclude that God must have created it. When discussing the *creation* or *existence* of the universe, avoid mentioning the *design* of the universe; this would be mixing cosmological arguments with TELEOLOGICAL (DESIGN) ARGUMENTS.

There are different versions of cosmological arguments, so avoid writing "the cosmological argument"; instead, refer to "(all) cosmological arguments", or to one cosmological argument in particular e.g. "Descartes' cosmological argument".

Cosmological arguments can be split into two types:

- CAUSAL ARGUMENTS suggest that everything has a cause, and the first cause of everything is God. Examples include the Kalam argument, Aquinas' first and second ways, and Descartes' argument.
- ARGUMENTS FROM CONTINGENCY suggest that the universe depends on something else for its existence, namely, God. Examples include Aquinas' 3rd way, and Leibniz's argument.

Unmoved mover

Aristotle outlines a cosmological argument in which he focuses on movement within the universe. He suggests that anything in motion must have a cause (a mover), and if we work backwards we'll find the first cause of everything will be an UNMOVED MOVER. This first cause can move other things, but is not moved by anything. The notion of an unmoved mover is one which recurs in several cosmological arguments.

Arguments from causation

Several strengths and criticisms – such as those listed below – can apply to various cosmological arguments from causation (but not necessarily to arguments from contingency).

Strength

- It does seem intuitively plausible that there must be a first cause of everything in the universe, and that cause must itself be uncaused.

Criticisms

- Even if there is a first cause, this does not prove that God exists; the universe could have been created by an evil, finitely powerful, non-omniscient being which has since died.
- Cosmological arguments begin from the idea that nothing can be uncaused – and then they suggest that God is uncaused; this is a contradiction.

Criticisms

- Hume and Russell suggest that cosmological arguments commit the FALLACY OF COMPOSITION – even if every event in the universe has a cause, that doesn't mean that all events have a single ultimate cause.
- Hume notes that it is odd that theists are unwilling to accept that the universe can be uncaused, but that they are willing to accept God as uncaused. If there can be an exception to the rule that 'everything has a cause' why can't the Big Bang be the exception?

Criticisms

- Mackie suggests that an infinite regress of causes is possible. He draws the analogy of a rope, and we may think it would need to be secured at the top or else it would fall down – but if it is an infinite rope, then there *is* no top. By this he means that every event in the universe has a cause – and the causes extend infinitely into the past: we don't need to posit a first cause, because infinite causes are possible.
- Russell (and physicists) point out that there are some uncaused events, such as quantum fluctuations at the sub-atomic level. These uncaused fluctuations are not God, so the universe could have been caused by an uncaused event which is not God.
- An alternative to the Big Bang theory *and* God as the first cause is the 'pulsating universe' theory – also known as the CYCLIC MODEL. This is where a Big Bang expands the universe, but then it begins to contract again into a Big Crunch, before the cycle begins again. This could have occurred infinitely into the past.

Response: This idea is criticised by theists and by some scientists who insist that there cannot be an infinite regress.

- Hume suggests that invoking a supernatural being to explain something in the natural world is not PARSIMONIOUS and is a flawed idea. OCKHAM'S RAZOR suggests that we should not posit more beings than are needed; we can explain the universe via the Big Bang, so there's no need to posit God.

Remember that even if all cosmological arguments fail to prove that God exists, this does not mean that God definitely *doesn't* exist – only that it hasn't been *proven*.

Aquinas' First and Second Ways

Overview

Key philosopher: Aquinas

Aquinas puts forward five ways of proving God's existence; his first three arguments are all cosmological arguments. The first two ways are ARGUMENTS FROM CAUSATION and are discussed here, while the third way is an ARGUMENT FROM CONTINGENCY (see p75).

Aquinas' first and second ways take a similar LOGICAL FORM, and are given together here for ease of analysis. In these two arguments, he borrows from Aristotle's notion of the UNMOVED MOVER. Aquinas argues that an INFINITE REGRESS of causation is not possible, and therefore there must be a first instance of movement (first way) or causation (second way); this of course is God.

Aquinas' first way is called the ARGUMENT FROM MOTION, and can be summarised as:

1. There are things in motion, or a state of change
2. Nothing can move or change itself – it needs something else to move or change it
3. If there were an infinite regress, then there'd be no first mover, so none of the other movers could move either

C. Therefore, there must be a first mover who is the source of all motion or change; this is God

Aquinas' second way is called the ARGUMENT FROM ATEMPORAL CAUSATION, and can be summarised as:

1. There are events occurring, each of which has a cause
2. Nothing can be the cause of itself – it needs something else to cause it
3. If there were an infinite regress, then there'd be no first cause, so none of the other events could become causes either

C. Therefore, there must be a first cause which is the source of all events and causes; this is God

Both of these arguments rely on the claim that things are occurring in the universe right now, and there must be some explanation for them. Aquinas offers God as the only plausible explanation of these events.

Because the formulation of Aquinas' first and second ways are so similar, the evaluation given below applies to both arguments.

Strengths	Criticisms
• It is plausible that almost all events have a cause or something to set them in motion.	• The arguments are contradictory: if nothing can move/change/cause itself, then how can God move/change/cause himself?

Also see the strengths and criticisms relating to various cosmological arguments (p69-70).

The Kalam Argument

Overview

Key philosopher: Al-Ghazali

The Kalam argument is a DEDUCTIVE COSMOLOGICAL ARGUMENT FROM TEMPORAL CAUSATION. Conceived of by medieval Islamic scholars including Al-Ghazali, the Kalam argument is formed in various ways by different philosophers. Generally speaking, the first three lines of the argument (the two premises, and the intermediate conclusion that the universe had a cause) remain the same, however the remainder of the argument varies depending on the author.

The Kalam argument can be summarised as:

1. Everything with a beginning has a cause
2. The universe had a beginning
3. Therefore, the universe had a cause
4. The cause of the universe must be uncaused, immutable, immaterial, eternal, and infinitely powerful
5. The cause of the universe must be either scientific or spiritual
6. Scientific explanations can't adequately explain the cause of the universe

C. Therefore, the cause of the universe must be spiritual: an uncaused, immutable, immaterial, eternal, and infinitely powerful God

Strengths

- The Kalam argument is a deductive argument so if it is successful, it proves the existence of God A PRIORI.
- It is plausible to say that the cause of the universe must be IMMATERIAL, because if it was material then it would be part of the universe.
- It is plausible to say that the cause of the universe must have existed outside of time (ETERNAL) when the universe – and time itself – were created.

Criticisms

- If the Kalam argument were an ABDUCTIVE ARGUMENT (an INFERENCE TO THE BEST EXPLANATION), then it could be reasonable to conclude that God is a more adequate explanation of the beginning of the universe than the Big Bang theory. But the Kalam argument is attempting to be a deductive argument – yet the conclusion is not logically ENTAILED by the premises; this means the argument fails.

Criticisms

- Premise 5 may be a FALSE DILEMMA: science and spirituality are not mutually exclusive, and there may be explanations which are neither scientific *nor* spiritual.
- Something could perhaps exist outside of time when it was creating the universe, but once time and the universe had been created, the creator began to exist inside of time (and he needn't live forever). So the creator of the universe might not be ETERNAL.
- Premise 6 is problematic: science has explained the Big Bang and how it occurred (and any remaining uncertainties might be explained in future – there needn't be a spiritual explanation).
- Some of the qualities in premise 4 are asserted without justification, for example IMMUTABILITY and being infinitely powerful; something exceptionally (but finitely) powerful could have created the universe, and then changed.

Also see the strengths and criticisms relating to various cosmological arguments (p69-70).

Descartes' Cosmological Argument

Overview | **Key philosopher:** Descartes

Descartes' cosmological argument is another ARGUMENT FROM CAUSATION. Unlike other cosmological arguments, Descartes' does not try to explain what caused the existence of the entire universe; he only tries to explain what caused his own existence. Descartes considers what could be the cause of his existence, and offers three possibilities:

(a) He is the cause of his own existence
(b) He has always existed (he has no cause)
(c) Something else has caused his existence

Descartes believes that it takes power to keep something existing from one moment to the next (he talks of being 'created anew each moment'). He dismisses (b) because even if he had always existed, he'd still need to discover what power 'creates him anew each moment'.

Descartes' trademark argument

Descartes maintains that if he is the cause of his own existence, then he is the cause of his own ideas too. This enables him to dismiss possibility (a) by intertwining it with his TRADEMARK ARGUMENT:

1. I am an imperfect being
2. I have the idea of a perfect, eternal, immutable, omnipotent, omniscient God
3. The cause of something must be more real and more perfect than the effect (the CAUSAL ADEQUACY PRINCIPLE)
4. Because I'm imperfect, I cannot be the cause of my idea of God
5. The idea of a perfect, eternal, immutable, omnipotent, omniscient God must be caused by something which is *actually* perfect, eternal, immutable, omnipotent, and omniscient

C. Therefore, a perfect, eternal, immutable, omnipotent, omniscient God exists, and is the cause of my idea

Descartes briefly considers whether he could be the cause of his idea of God (i.e. he made it up himself) and whether he brought himself into own existence. However, Descartes dismisses this because only God could be the cause of the idea, and only God could 'create Descartes anew each moment', and Descartes knows that he is not God.

Having dismissed the possibilities that he has caused his own existence or that he's always existed, Descartes presents his COSMOLOGICAL ARGUMENT which can be summarised as:

1. Something is the cause of my existence
2. Either the cause of my existence is caused by something else, or it is uncaused
3. If it is caused by something else, then either that thing is caused by something else, or it is uncaused
4. There can be no infinite regress, so it will eventually reach an ultimate cause which is uncaused

C. Therefore, the ultimate cause of my existence is God

Because Descartes intertwined his cosmological argument with his trademark argument, criticisms of his trademark argument are indirectly criticisms of his cosmological argument.

Strengths

- It is possible that Descartes' idea of God came directly from God himself, like a trademark, as Descartes suggests.
- Many people across the world and throughout history have had the idea of God – even atheists have the idea of God.

Criticisms

- The causal adequacy principle is flawed. There is not a spectrum of reality; things are either real or not real. And it is not the case that the cause of something must be more real or as real as the effect – the (unreal) idea of werewolves can cause (real) fear in me.

Response: Even if the causal adequacy principle fails, it is still legitimate to ask what caused Descartes' existence, and to work backwards towards a first cause.

- It is quite possible for someone to make up the idea of God by themselves; it needn't come from God. People have made up the ideas of dragons, goblins and unicorns, so could make up God too.
- We do not need something to sustain our existence and 'create us anew each moment', so something could have created Descartes, then ceased to exist.

Also see the strengths and criticisms relating to various cosmological arguments (p69-70).

Aquinas' Third Way

Overview

Key philosopher: Aquinas

Aquinas' third way is a cosmological ARGUMENT FROM CONTINGENCY which states that God is a NECESSARY BEING, while everything else in the universe is merely CONTINGENT.

Aquinas argues that everything in the universe could have turned out differently (or not existed at all): the universe is contingent, but God is not. His third way can be summarised as:

1. Things in the universe are contingent
2. If a thing is contingent, there are times when it does not exist
3. Therefore, if all things are contingent, there are times when nothing exists
4. Something cannot come from nothing
5. If there was once a time when nothing existed, then there would still be nothing now (but this is false)

C. Therefore, there must be something necessary (God) on which contingent things rely

Aquinas' argument rests on the idea that the universe is contingent, and so if we work backwards in time, there would be a time when the universe did not exist. He reasons that contingent things cannot cause themselves to exist, therefore there must be something necessary to have caused the existence of our (contingent) universe, and that something is God.

Aquinas discusses whether a necessary being could rely on something else for its existence, but he rightly dismisses the idea, because a necessary being which depends on something else is contradictory.

Strengths

- It seems true that the universe is contingent, and that something cannot come from nothing.
- Even people who believe in the Big Bang might still ask what caused the Big Bang; it seems implausible that it was uncaused or that it caused itself.

Criticisms

- Hume and Russell point out that there is no such thing as 'necessary existence' or a 'necessary being' because "God does not exist" is not a contradiction.
- Even if Aquinas proves that there was a necessary being which was the first cause of the universe, this would not prove that he has features such as omnipotence, omniscience, omnibenevolence, and so on.

Criticisms

- Premise 2 states that contingent things exist for a while, then cease to exist, but Aquinas was not aware of the principle known as the 'conservation of mass' which states that matter is not created or destroyed, only changed from one form to another. So even when stars 'die' or when energy is released as heat, the energy/mass still exists within the universe; nothing truly ceases to exist.
- Mackie argues that it is illogical for Aquinas to move from premise 2 to premise 3. Even if everything in the universe doesn't exist at some point, that does not mean that all those occasions coincide with one another. One thing in the universe can 'die' while others continue to exist.

Leibniz's Cosmological Argument

Overview

Key philosopher: Leibniz

Leibniz's cosmological argument is an ARGUMENT FROM CONTINGENCY. He asks why there is a universe, rather than nothing at all; his answer is that only a NECESSARY BEING could have created a (CONTINGENT) universe, and that necessary being is of course God.

In Leibniz's original text, he merges his cosmological argument with a TELEOLOGICAL (DESIGN) ARGUMENT (he asks why there is a universe, and why it is the way it is). You must avoid blurring arguments like this in the exam. Our focus here is solely on the *existence / cause* of the universe, not the *design* of the universe.

Principle of sufficient reason

Leibniz bases his cosmological argument on the PRINCIPLE OF SUFFICIENT REASON (PSR). This principle states that any CONTINGENT fact must have an explanation for why it is that way, and not another way.

Leibniz argues that a necessary being is the only possible explanation for why our universe exists. His argument can be summarised as:

1. All contingent facts must have an adequate explanation (PSR)
2. (implied) It is a contingent fact that the (contingent) universe exists
3. Therefore the existence of the (contingent) universe must have an adequate explanation
4. The existence of the (contingent) universe cannot be explained by something contingent
5. The existence of the (contingent) universe must be explained by something necessary

C. Therefore, a necessary being exists

Strengths

- It seems plausible to suggest that the universe is probably contingent; there could have been a different universe, or no universe at all.
- If Leibniz's argument is correct and a necessary being exists, then God is possibly the necessary being.

Criticisms

- The PSR is merely asserted: there is no justification for why all contingent things need an explanation for why they are the way they are. Many things in the universe occur due to random chance; perhaps the existence of the universe itself is due to random chance.
- Maybe some things require no explanation or reason. Russell, Hume and others argue that the universe doesn't require an explanation; it 'just is'.
- Hume and Russell point out that there is no such thing as a 'necessary being' because "God does not exist" is not a contradiction; all beings are contingent.
- If something could exist necessarily, then why must it be God? It could be the universe itself: the universe could exist necessarily even if its features are contingent. The Big Bang may be a necessary event.
- Assuming something *can* exist necessarily, there would be no way to tell the difference between a God (or a universe) which exists necessarily, and one which only exists contingently.
- The PSR only tells us that contingent things need an explanation – it does not state or imply that necessary things *don't* need an explanation; it is reasonable to seek an explanation of why a necessary God exists, just as it is reasonable to seek an explanation of why the contingent universe exists.
- It is not clear that the only explanation for the existence of the universe is a *necessary* being. A contingent (but exceptionally powerful) being could create a universe.
- Premise 2 can be challenged: it could be a necessary fact that the contingent universe exists, in which case, the existence of the universe might not require an explanation.
- Leibniz does not conclude that it is a *necessary* fact that "a necessary being explains the existence of the universe" so, by the PSR, we should seek an explanation of *why* a necessary being explains the existence of the universe.
- Even if we accept Leibniz's conclusion that a necessary being exists, this does not prove that it is God, with the attributes we usually associate with him, such as OMNISCIENCE, OMNIPOTENCE and so on.

Religious Language

Overview

Key philosopher: Wittgenstein

We use language to express ourselves on a day-to-day basis, and we are able to do so because of the shared meanings of words which we use. But communicating about religious matters can be tricky because it may not always be clear what people mean by religious statements. For example, people disagree about what God's attributes are (see p30) and even about what particular attributes mean (for example, whether OMNIPOTENCE means the ability to do the LOGICALLY IMPOSSIBLE (see p33)).

Some philosophers of religious language suggest that there is something special or different about religious language compared to other language. There is also disagreement about whether religious language is meaningful at all.

The nature of religious language

Religious language (and perhaps by implication, religious belief) can be confusing and contradictory when we consider statements such as "God is the father, the son and the holy spirit", or the idea that God is IMMATERIAL, yet he moulded Adam out of clay and blew life into him.

Language and meaning

Generally, speakers of English understand the meanings of the words they use and hear every day, and do not need to discuss with others what is meant by a particular word. We recognise sentences which do not make sense, but there are different ways in which something might not make sense to us. Consider the following sentences:

(a) The droghte of Marche hath perced to the roote*

(b) Frog of it very the annual use but of make be

(c) I hear a non-existent hatred blistering

Sentence (a) does not make (complete) sense to us today because it was written over 500 years ago and our language and spelling has changed during that time; not all of the words in the sentence are familiar to us.

---

* Chaucer, G. (c.1476) The Canterbury Tales, line 2

Sentence (b) uses words we understand, but it doesn't make sense because the words are in the wrong order; it is ungrammatical. Sentence (c) uses familiar words and is grammatical, but the way the concepts are used is problematic and confusing (how can hatred blister? How can something be heard if it is non-existent?)

When philosophers discuss religious language and claim that it isn't (or is) meaningful, it is usually the third type of meaningfulness which they are referring to – i.e. they are making claims about whether the concepts in the sentence are being used in a consistent and non-contradictory way.

Cognitivism and non-cognitivism

You may recall COGNITIVISM and NON-COGNITIVISM from your study of ethical language (meta-ethics) for Paper 1. These approaches to religious language are similar to the approaches to ethical language.

• *Cognitivism:* Propositions must have a truth-value in order to be meaningful.	• *Non-cognitivism:* Statements can still be meaningful without having a truth-value.

Cognitivists maintain that when people make religious statements such as "Jesus is risen" or "God lives in all of us" they are simply articulating their beliefs; religious claims generally do not have a TRUTH-VALUE.

A truth-value means that the statement is either true or false (it doesn't matter which). The statements "a bike has two wheels" and "a bike has two thousand wheels" both have a truth-value (one is true; the other is false). On the other hand, "cheese is delicious" and "God walks beside me" are not the sorts of statements which can be true or false.

Cognitivists and non-cognitivists agree that the statements about bikes are meaningful. However, they disagree on the statements about cheese and God: non-cognitivists say the statements are meaningful, whereas cognitivists say they are not factually meaningful.

Language games

Wittgenstein argues that language is like a game, with rules about meaning which only particular groups of people fully understand. For example, if someone who is not a parent or midwife listens to people discussing childbirth, they will probably not understand what is meant by 'meconium', 'colostrum' or an 'Apgar score'.

Wittgenstein suggests that if religious statements are understood by religious people (people in the 'religious language' game) then they are meaningful. Atheists may pick apart the statements and find nothing factually substantive, but the statements are nonetheless meaningful to believers. Wittgenstein argues that science and religion are different language games, and so trying to understand religion in a scientific way (such as through VERIFICATION or FALSIFICATION) is futile.

Verification

Overview	**Key philosophers:** Vienna Circle, Ayer

Verificationism is a COGNITIVIST approach to religious language. Verificationists suggest that religious statements are not meaningful because they are not VERIFIABLE (they cannot be proven true). This is an EMPIRICIST approach because it relies on the possibility of physical proof.

Logical positivism

LOGICAL POSITIVISM is a theory which maintains that if language is to be meaningful, it must stick to discussing things which could (theoretically) be proven true. Once people start discussing metaphysical concepts which go beyond human experience (such as souls, God, Heaven) it is problematic.

Ayer is a logical positivist who proposes the VERIFICATION PRINCIPLE which states that:

A proposition is meaningful if and only if it is either (a) or (b):

(a) ANALYTIC

(b) VERIFIABLE IN PRINCIPLE

If it is neither (a) nor (b) then it is factually meaningless

The VIENNA CIRCLE is a group of logical positivists who were writing in Vienna, Austria during the 1920s and 30s. They too suggest that propositions are analytic, verifiable in principle, or meaningless.

Analytic statements such as 'Vixens are foxes' are true by definition, because once you understand the meaning of the words, you know A PRIORI that it is true. According to Ayer, whilst analytic truths tell us trivialities, propositions which are verifiable in principle are FACTUALLY SIGNIFICANT, and can tell us something SUBSTANTIVE about the world.

The verification principle can be applied to statements as a test of meaningfulness. Logical positivists would reach the following conclusions about these statements:

(a) Wolves are canine	Analytic	Meaningful
(b) There's a wolf in my bedroom	Verifiable	Meaningful
(c) There's a wolf in the centre of the sun	Verifiable	Meaningful
(d) Wolves ripple in the cellar of mentality	Not analytic or verifiable	Meaningless

Statement (d) is not analytic and it is not verifiable; therefore, it is a PSEUDO-PROPOSITION. A lot of poetry and metaphorical language is factually meaningless according to the logical positivists; even if it sounds beautiful and we understand what it is supposed to symbolise, it is not FACTUALLY MEANINGFUL.

The logical positivists suggest that religious language is not factually meaningful either: even though many people understand what is meant by religious statements, they do not make claims which can be VERIFIED IN PRINCIPLE.

Verifiable in principle

Saying that something is verifiable in principle means that we know what empirical evidence it would take to prove the statement true. For example, the statement 'There is a wolf in the centre of the sun' could be proven true by flying to the centre of the sun and finding the wolf. It doesn't matter that this check could not *actually* take place; all that matters is that the statement could, *in principle*, be checked and proven true. Whenever logical positivists discuss verifiability, they are referring to verifiability in principle.

Religious language is not verifiable

Ayer and the Vienna Circle argue that religious statements are meaningless because they are not analytic, and they are not verifiable even in principle.

Statements such as 'God exists', 'souls reside in Heaven' or 'God is the Father, the Son and the Holy Ghost' are not verifiable because they go beyond the sphere of human experience, and we don't know what evidence it would take to prove them, nor how (even in principle) they could be verified. Therefore they are factually meaningless.

Strength

- The verification principle is a robust way of determining whether a statement can be proven (in principle).

Criticisms

- The verification principle is too extreme, and dismisses much of our language as meaningless, perhaps including aesthetic statements ("Sandra is beautiful"), ethical statements ("killing is wrong"), poetic / metaphorical statements ("time is the fire in which we burn"). Without these sorts of statements, our language would be dull and emotionless.

Response: We don't have to stop using this sort of language; only to admit that it is not factually meaningful language.

- Some religious statements do seem verifiable in principle, for example "angels exist" could be proven true by seeing and speaking with an angel.

Criticisms

- There are many scientific statements which cannot be verified but which are meaningful nonetheless, e.g. 'there are more stars than there are grains of sand on Earth'.

Response: This claim can be verified *in principle*, namely by counting all the grains of sand, and counting all the stars.

- The verification principle is not analytically true (because just understanding the meanings of the words doesn't demonstrate its truth), nor is it verifiable (there is no way to prove it). So the verification principle, by its own definition, is meaningless! The principle is self-defeating which makes it highly problematic.
- Perhaps it is not verification, but FALSIFICATION which is the criterion of meaningfulness (see p87).
- It is possible that some religious statements are ESCHATOLOGICALLY VERIFIABLE (see p84).

Eschatological Verification

Overview

Key philosopher: Hick

ESCHATOLOGICAL VERIFICATION is a response to the COGNITIVISTS' claim that religious statements are not meaningful because they are not VERIFIABLE.

Hick agrees with Ayer and the other logical positivists that only verifiable (FACTUALLY SIGNIFICANT) statements are meaningful. However, Hick argues that religious statements *are* meaningful because they are indeed verifiable.

Verification after death

Hick argues that religious statements are eschatologically verifiable. 'Eschatological' means 'end of life', so eschatological verification is proving something at the end of one's life. The suggestion is that there are at least some religious statements which can be verified after death – for example, if there is an afterlife, then we will verify the statement "there is an afterlife".

Hick defines verifiability in terms of 'removing rational doubt': if you arrive in Heaven, there can be no rational doubt that an afterlife exists. Thus Hick suggests that religious statements are verifiable and therefore meaningful.

The Celestial City

To demonstrate his argument about eschatological verification, Hick puts forward a parable about the Celestial City:

Two men are walking on the same road. The first man believes it leads to the Celestial City; the other believes it leads nowhere, but both men walk on the road as it is the only road there is. Their experiences on the road are largely similar, except the first man interprets the trials and obstacles on the road as preparation for what awaits at the Celestial City; the other man sees no such significance in the obstacles. When they reach the final corner of the road, they'll turn it and see which one of them was correct about where the road leads.	The parable is a metaphor: the road is our lives, the two men represent atheists and theists, and the Celestial City is Heaven or the afterlife. Hick argues that only one of the men can be correct about where the road leads, but they won't know who is correct until they reach the end of the road.

In this way, Hick attempts to demonstrate that if the road reaches the Celestial City, both men will realise that the Celestial City does indeed exist; it will be verified.

Replicas and the afterlife

In order for me to verify the existence of Heaven, I will need to be in Heaven after I die. But how could I be in Heaven, while my body and brain are decomposing on Earth? If 'I' arrive in Heaven, then what exactly has arrived in Heaven?

To answer this, Hick puts forward a thought experiment to show how the afterlife could be possible. Some of the arguments in favour of SUBSTANCE DUALISM (see p96) can also support Hick's suggestion that a person can be in Heaven even though their body remains on Earth.

Hick's thought experiment has three stages:

1. A person disappears in London, while an exact replica of him appears in New York; he is in every way identical to the one who disappeared in London.
2. A person 'dies' in London, and their corpse remains there, while an exact replica of him appears in New York; he is in every way identical to the one who 'died' in London.
3. A person dies in London, and their corpse remains there, while an exact replica of him appears in the afterlife; he is in every way identical to the one who died in London.

Hick suggests that in each scenario, we would consider the replica to be the same person as the one who disappears / dies. From these three thought experiments, Hick believes he has shown how PERSONAL CONTINUITY into the afterlife is (LOGICALLY) POSSIBLE.

Hick argues that when someone is in Heaven, it will remove all rational doubt about whether it *really* is the afterlife. This will happen because:

- We'll finally understand our purpose and destiny given to us by God
- We'll encounter Jesus Christ

Hick believes that everyone will eventually make it to Heaven (recall his SOUL-MAKING THEODICY – see p53), but even if it only happened to *some* people, the claim would still have been verified, which would make the claim 'God exists' meaningful.

Strengths

- It does seem possible that a person's spirit or soul could continue into the afterlife even though their body has died.
- If there is an afterlife, then at least some religious statements such as "there is an afterlife" will be verified.

Criticisms

- Hick asserts that when in the afterlife, we'll encounter Jesus Christ / God, but it is not clear that we will; the afterlife may be overseen by a God which is not the Christian God, or there could be an afterlife without any God at all.
- Hick suggests that when we encounter Jesus Christ / God, we'll recognise them, but it is not clear that we would definitely recognise them: how can we recognise someone whom we have never met before?
- Hick does not address the idea that the afterlife may not just consist of Heaven, but also of Hell, purgatory, limbo and other possibilities. If someone dies and goes to limbo, then they might not be able to verify any religious statements.

Criticisms

- A problem with the replica thought experiments is that a replica is not the original person; not everyone would agree that the replica is the same person as the one who died or disappeared.
- A replica appearing on Earth can be in every way identical to me (my body and mind) but a replica who appears in Heaven is not identical to me. Most conceptions of the afterlife say that IMMATERIAL souls reside in Heaven, and dead bodies stay on Earth. The thing which arrives in Heaven is not identical to me (it doesn't have my body), therefore it is not me.
- It is not clear that a non-physical mind / soul could be separated from the physical body or replicated in Heaven; humans might be a purely physical substance (see problems with SUBSTANCE DUALISM p100-107).
- Even if I die and realise that I am in Heaven, there are many religious statements which I can't verify, such as "God is the father, the son and the holy spirit", "God is omniscient", and "God is the creator of the universe" – so even after death, many religious statements are still unverifiable and thus according to the logical positivists, meaningless.

Falsification: The University Debate

Overview | **Key philosophers:** Flew, Hare, Mitchell

In the 1950s, three philosophers had a debate about falsification through articles written in the journal *University* – this came to be known as the University Debate. Each philosopher puts forward their argument in the form of a parable.

Flew: The Invisible Gardener

Flew is a COGNITIVIST: he believes that only FALSIFIABLE propositions are FACTUALLY MEANINGFUL. (Like the logical positivists, Flew believes that factually meaningful propositions divulge SUBSTANTIVE facts about the world.) Flew's focus on factual meaningfulness is similar to that of the logical positivists, but Flew maintains that it is falsifiability – not VERIFIABILITY – which makes a proposition meaningful.

Falsifiability

For a belief to be falsifiable, the believer must know what evidence it would take to disprove it. For example, say I believe I will win the lottery tomorrow. I can conceive of some evidence which would falsify my belief: if my numbers are not chosen tomorrow, I will accept that my belief was wrong. Since my belief is falsifiable, it is factually meaningful according to Flew.

If tomorrow comes and my numbers don't come up, but I stubbornly cling to the idea that I have *really* won the lottery – I ignore the evidence from the TV, internet, newspapers and other people – then my belief is not falsifiable, and it is therefore meaningless.

The parable

Flew presents his argument in a parable originally told by John Wisdom so it is sometimes referred to as "Wisdom's gardener". Flew does not give the men names, but names are given here to make the parable easier to follow. The parable can be summarised as:

> Two explorers – Arthur and Bruce – are out walking when they come across a garden; Bruce says "a gardener must come here and tend to these beautiful flowers". Arthur says he doesn't think there is a gardener, because there are lots of messy weeds around the flowers. Bruce replies that the gardener must have left some weeds there on purpose.
>
> To discover whether there is a gardener, the two men set up camp for several days – but they see no gardener. Finally Arthur says, "I told you there

was no gardener" – but Bruce responds that the gardener must be invisible. So the men set up an infra-red camera and an electric fence, but still no gardener is detected. Arthur is satisfied he has proven that no gardener exists, but Bruce stubbornly claims that the gardener must be invisible, intangible, undetectable by infra-red, and immune to electric shocks. Exasperated, Arthur asks Bruce "But what is the difference between an invisible, intangible gardener who leaves some weeds among the flowers – and no gardener at all?"

The parable is an analogy for belief in God: Bruce is the believer and Arthur is the atheist, while the invisible, intangible gardener is God. Some people also suggest that the weeds represent evil and chaos in the world, while the flowers represent goodness and order.

Flew's parable is intended to show that theists are not open to their beliefs being falsified, because whenever they are presented with evidence that God doesn't exist, they just modify their belief in order to maintain that God does exist. This can be seen in the table below.

Theist's claim	**Atheist's criticism**	**Theist's modified claim**
God exists	No one's ever seen, heard or felt him	God is invisible, INCORPOREAL, and silent
God is omnipotent	But he can't make a stone too big for him to lift	God is omnipotent but doesn't do the logically impossible
Heaven exists	No one has ever shown proof of it	It exists, but it's not possible to return to Earth from Heaven (except for Christ)
God loves humans	But humans suffer terribly at the hands of each other and natural disasters	God gave us free will to harm each other, and natural disasters strengthen our souls
God created animals as we see them today	Evolution suggests dinosaurs and other creatures have changed over times and some have gone extinct	God created prehistoric animals and monitored their evolution, FINE-TUNING THEM towards humans

Death by a thousand qualifications

If someone makes a claim, but then whenever they are presented with evidence to the contrary, they just alter their claim rather than give up on it, then their claim suffers "DEATH BY A THOUSAND QUALIFICATIONS".

Flew suggests that if a theist makes the claim "God exists" but she cannot conceive of any evidence which would falsify her claim, then her claim is factually meaningless. Flew suggests that most (if not all) religious statements are meaningless in this way because the speakers are not open to their statements being falsified.

Foresight and falsification

Flew's claim is that unless a speaker knows what would falsify their belief, then it is meaningless. The problem with this is that people might not be able to predict what will falsify their belief. Consider a married couple, who both have a strong belief that God exists (see panel, right).

Andrew says "I believe God exists" and he can't conceive of anything which would convince him that his belief is false.

His wife, Kerry, says "I believe God exists" but she thinks to herself that if her children died horrifically in spite of her prayers, this would demonstrate that her belief in God is false.

Suppose that sadly, Andrew and Kerry's children *do* die horrifically in spite of their parents' prayers. But surprisingly, Kerry finds her faith unshaken and she believes that the children's souls are with God in Heaven – meanwhile, Andrew finds his faith shaken to the core and he becomes an atheist.

Thus, Andrew couldn't conceive of what might falsify his belief, but it *was* actually falsified, whereas Kerry *could* conceive of what would falsify her belief – and yet when this occurred, her belief was *not* falsified. This shows that *thinking* your belief is falsifiable differs from a belief *actually* being falsifiable, and it is not possible to predict whether a belief *really* could be falsified for a particular person. So falsifiability is not an adequate criterion of meaningfulness.

Strengths	Criticisms
• It seems right to say that a speaker (such as 'Bruce') who keeps modifying his assertions in the face of compelling evidence has a very weak argument. • Strong arguments are able to say that such-and-such evidence would disprove the theory; this helps others know what to look for if they are trying to falsify the theory. If people look for evidence to falsify the theory but find none, then the theory is strengthened.	• Flew does not give us any good reason to subscribe to his theory of falsification: *why* must a theory be falsifiable in order to be meaningful? • There may be many people who believe in God but can conceive of evidence which would falsify their belief (like 'Kerry', above); Flew must be forced to accept that these people hold meaningful religious beliefs.

Criticisms

- Some atheists are as committed to their views as theists are, and no amount of evidence will convince them that there *is* a God.
- It is impossible to know whether people's beliefs are factually meaningful without questioning them about possible evidence which would falsify it.
- It is odd to think that two people can both have the same belief (such as "there is a God"), and one of them is factually meaningful, while the other is meaningless (because the first can conceive of evidence which would falsify their belief, but the second cannot).
- Swinburne argues that there are many meaningful but unfalsifiable statements, such as the statement that toys come alive and dance around when no one is looking, without leaving any trace.
- Hare puts forward a criticism suggesting that people can have unfalsifiable beliefs ('bliks') which are nonetheless meaningful (see p91).
- Mitchell puts forward a criticism suggesting that people can choose to have (meaningful) beliefs even when the evidence is inconclusive (see p91).

Hare: The Paranoid Student

Hare's argument is intended to be a criticism of Flew's theory of falsificationism as a criterion of meaning. Hare takes a NON-COGNITIVIST approach to religious language: he suggests that statements can be meaningful even if they don't have a TRUTH-VALUE, and they are just expressions of feelings.

Hare argues that even though a religious statement may not be easily falsifiable, it can still be meaningful. His parable can be summarised as:

A paranoid lunatic is a student at university, and is convinced all his professors are plotting to murder him. Despite his friends introducing him to many mild-mannered and kindly professors, the paranoid student maintains that the professors are cunning tricksters, pretending to be mild-mannered and kindly in order to cover their tracks, when they are really plotting to murder him.

The paranoid student cannot conceive of any evidence which would convince him that his belief is false. If we adhere to Flew's falsifiability criterion, then that the paranoid student's statement "my professors are plotting to kill me" is meaningless. Hare sees this as absurd.

Bliks

Hare invents the word 'BLIK' to mean a statement which is believed so deeply that the speaker isn't open to it being falsified – but which is still meaningful. The paranoid student has an incorrect blik (that his professors are plotting to kill him). Hare argues that when theists say "God exists" they are putting forward their blik; they're expressing an opinion rather than making an assertion – and it is meaningful even if it's not falsifiable.

Strength

- The student (and theists) are making meaningful claims inasmuch as they mean something to the speaker, and we understand what they mean.

Criticisms

- Even if we concede that many religious statements are expressions of opinions, this does not show that they are *factually* meaningful. Just like other opinions such as "bacon is disgusting" or "yellow is the best colour" are meaningful because we understand them, they are not FACTUALLY SUBSTANTIVE, so Flew's argument still stands.

Criticisms

- Flew points out that when theists make claims like "God exists" they are *not* merely expressing opinions: they are trying to make TRUTH-APT assertions – factual statements about the world; if religion is really just a blik then it is not much of a religion at all.
- Drawing an analogy between a theist and a paranoid lunatic is an odd way to suggest that theists' beliefs are rational and meaningful: instead it suggests that theists are lunatics who cling to their belief despite all rational evidence to the contrary.

Mitchell: The Partisan

Mitchell's parable is intended to be a criticism of Flew's theory of falsification as a criterion of meaning. He puts forward a parable about a partisan. His parable can be summarised as:

During a time of war in an occupied country, a member of the resistance (the partisan) meets a stranger who deeply impresses him. The partisan is utterly convinced of the stranger's sincerity, and trusts him. After that, the partisan sometimes sees the stranger helping the resistance, while at other times he helps enemy soldiers and is dressed as one of them. The partisan remains committed to believing the sincerity of the stranger, and that he is on the side of the resistance. The partisan's friends say the stranger is not on their side, and ask him "what would he have to do for you to admit that you were wrong?"

Mitchell's partisan parable is supposed to show that religious claims aren't just expressions of feelings (or 'bliks'); they are substantive assertions about the world.

In Mitchell's parable, the partisan does occasionally doubt his belief in the sincerity of the stranger, but upon further reflection, he always chooses to believe that the stranger is sincere. Similarly, theists do doubt their faith at times. They are not just stubbornly ignoring evidence against their beliefs; theists acknowledge the evidence against their beliefs, but choose to continue to believe.

Neither the partisan nor theists have seen *conclusive* evidence which falsifies their beliefs, and so continuing to trust and have faith in their beliefs is quite reasonable. It's not that the partisan and the theists have *unfalsifiable* beliefs – it's that they have beliefs which have not (yet) been falsified.

Strengths	**Criticisms**
• It's fair to say that theists haven't been shown *conclusive* proof that there is no God, and so continuing to believe might be reasonable rather than irrational. • It is possible for a belief to be falsifiable, yet never be falsified despite quite compelling evidence against it.	• The partisan (and arguably, theists) have been shown fairly compelling evidence that their beliefs are flawed, and so we can wonder just how conclusive the evidence must be in order to convince them to abandon their faith.

Metaphysics of Mind Overview

What is the mind?

- Monism and dualism
- Phenomenology, qualia and intentionality

Substance dualism

- Argument from indivisibility (Descartes)
- Argument from conceivability (Descartes)
  - Masked man fallacy
- The problem of other minds
  - The argument from analogy (Mill)
  - Argument to the best explanation
- Mind-body interaction
  - Interactionist dualism
  - Epiphenomenalist dualism

Property dualism

- Philosophical zombie argument (Chalmers)
- Mary's black and white room (Jackson)

Physicalism

- Behaviourism
  - Hard and soft behaviourism
  - Multiple realisability
- Mind-brain type identity theory and mind-brain token identity theory
  - Argument from conceivability (Putnam)
- Eliminative materialism (the Churchlands)
  - Rejection of folk psychology
  - Inverted qualia argument

Functionalism

- Mental states can be explained in terms of functions
  - Turing test
  - Chinese room (Searle)
  - Chinese mind argument (Block)

Substances

Overview

A SUBSTANCE is a thing that can exist on its own, independently of anything else. Philosophers disagree about how many substances there are in the universe; their answer to this question informs their beliefs about whether the mind is the same thing as the brain.

Generally, philosophers say that there are either two substances, or just one substance.

• MONISTS suggest that there is only one substance in the universe.	• DUALISTS suggest that there are two substances in the universe.

Dualists suggest that the two substances in existence are mind and matter. Matter is a physical substance which all physical things are made from, including tables, asteroids, trees, and electrons. Dualists see the mind as a non-physical substance which is capable of having thoughts, emotions, and other mental experiences.

Monists typically suggest that the only substance in existence is matter; these philosophers are known as MATERIALISTS. (Some philosophers (IMMATERIALISTS) suggest that the only substance in existence is the mind – and nothing physical exists. So not all monists are materialists.)

Metaphysics of Mind: *What is the nature of the mind?*			
Monism: Only one substance exists			**Dualism:** Two substances exist
Mind	**Matter**		**Mind and matter**
Immaterialism Only the mind exists	**Physicalism** Everything is physical or supervenes on the physical	**Property dualism:** The mind is not reducible to the brain	**Substance dualism:** Two substances exist; the mind is a different substance from the brain

Functionalism
Mental properties can be understood in terms of functions

Physicalist theories:		
Eliminative materialism Mental properties do not exist	**Behaviourism** Mental properties can be understood in terms of behaviour	**Identity theory** Mental properties are identical to physical (brain) properties

What is the Mind?

Overview

METAPHYSICS in general tries to answer two central questions: What exists? And what is it like? In our everyday lives, we assume that minds exist, but we can find it more difficult to articulate exactly what we mean by the mind, and what the mind is like.

There are a number of features which are said to be unique to the mind. It is suggested that at least some mental states possess the following properties, many of which are related to one another:

Qualia Qualia are the way things look, feel, taste, smell and sound to us; the unique way an experience seems. For example, the smell of a rose, the taste of a burger, the feeling of grief. Only a mind can experience a quale. Qualia are said to be INFALLIBLE, INEFFABLE, IMMEDIATELY ACCESSIBLE, and to have an INTRINSIC NATURE. They are a type of non-INTENTIONAL PHENOMENOLOGICAL event which are INTROSPECTIVELY ACCESSIBLE.	**Phenomenology** Phenomenology is the study of conscious experiences from a first-personal point of view (such as thoughts, emotions, bodily sensations and QUALIA). Phenomenological experiences are subjective, INFALLIBLE, INTENTIONAL, and IMMEDIATELY ACCESSIBLE. All or at least some mental states have phenomenal properties.
Intentionality My thoughts, beliefs, hopes (etc) are directed at something; they are 'intent' upon something. I can't just hope – I must hope *something in particular*, such as "I hope it's sunny tomorrow".	**Infallibility** It is said that my thoughts are INFALLIBLE – I cannot be mistaken about them. If I *think* I'm wishing for cake, then I definitely am wishing for cake.

To say that mental states are intentional doesn't mean they are created on purpose, it means that they represent something; they have some propositional content.	It's not possible that I think I'm wishing for cake when really I am remembering a time I saw an elephant.
Introspective access I can access my thoughts easily in a way that you cannot access my thoughts; my thoughts are first-personal. If I am thinking about cats, then I am NON-INFERENTIALLY aware of this, whereas if *you* are thinking about cats then I wouldn't know it automatically; I would have to infer it based on your behaviour.	**Immediate access** I am immediately aware of my thoughts. If I am thinking about hippos, then I am aware of this thought instantly; I don't have to wait a while until I realise what I'm thinking. My mind activities are immediately accessible to me through INTROSPECTION (merely thinking about them).
Ineffability QUALIA (and probably some other mind activities) are INEFFABLE in that they cannot be described with words. For example, it is impossible to describe green to a congenitally blind person, or to explain the taste of a lemon to someone who has never eaten fruit.	**Intrinsic nature** Mind activities – and QUALIA in particular – are said to have an intrinsic nature, meaning that they cannot be broken down into parts. For example, the taste of an orange or the pain of being stabbed cannot be divided into sections.

Substance Dualism

Overview — **Key philosopher:** Descartes

Descartes is perhaps the founder of SUBSTANCE DUALISM – also known as CARTESIAN DUALISM. He argues that there are two SUBSTANCES in the universe: the mental and the physical. The mind is a mental (non-physical) substance whereas the body and brain are physical substances.

According to Descartes, an inanimate object such as a table is a purely physical substance, a mind is a purely mental substance, and a human is a COMPOSITE SUBSTANCE – it is a mental *and* a physical substance.

Bodies, brains, minds, souls

Descartes often uses the terms 'mind' and 'soul' interchangeably. He also sometimes uses 'brain' and 'body' interchangeably. For example, at times he writes that the mind is not the same thing as the body, but no one genuinely suggests that the mind is the (entire) body. A more common claim is that the mind is the *brain*.

In order to avoid ATTACKING A STRAW MAN, we should try to interpret Descartes' arguments in the strongest way possible. This textbook sometimes exchanges 'soul' for 'mind', and 'body' for 'brain' in order to generously strengthen Descartes' arguments.

Intermingling thesis

Descartes writes that although the mind and body are distinct substances, they are INTERMINGLED, because one is aware of bodily sensations such as hunger, heat and pain. Descartes notes that he is aware when his body is injured, not just because he observes the blood or bruises, but because he *feels* the pain. He contrasts this with the captain of a ship who merely observes the damage without feeling it.

This intermingling of mind and body does not mean that the mind is distributed throughout the entire body. For example, if my leg is severed, I don't lose a part of my mind as well. This is because the mind and body are distinct substances.

In putting forward this intermingling thesis, Descartes sidesteps any criticisms which point out that my mind and body seem very much linked to one another.

Proofs that the mind is not the brain

Descartes puts forward several 'proofs' that the mind and the brain are different substances from one another. His arguments rely on a version of Leibniz's Law of Identity:

Leibniz's Law of Identity:
If A is the same thing as B, then whatever is true of A is also true of B.

Due to Leibniz's Law, if Descartes can show that there is something which is true of the mind which is not true of the brain, this should demonstrate that the mind is not the brain. Descartes gives several differences between the mind and brain:

(a) The mind can think; the brain/body cannot.	(b) The mind is non-extended (non-physical); the brain is extended (physical).	(c) The body is divisible; the mind is indivisible (ARGUMENT FROM INDIVISIBILITY).
(d) I can doubt that I have a body; I can't doubt that I have a mind (ARGUMENT FROM DUBITABILITY).	(e) I can conceive of myself as existing without a brain/body, but not without a mind (ARGUMENT FROM CONCEIVABILITY).	

Several of these proofs BEG THE QUESTION, because they assume that the mind and brain are different – an assumption which a physicalist would challenge. For example, a physicalist would maintain that the brain *can* think (a), and that the mind *is* a physical thing, namely the brain (b).

Proofs (c), (d) and (e) are more convincing than (a) and (b); the ARGUMENT FROM INDIVISIBILITY is considered on p105; the ARGUMENTS FROM DUBITABILITY and CONCEIVABILITY are very similar, and are considered together on p101.

Features of the mind

In addition to the proofs which Descartes puts forward, we can also add that the features of the mind on p95 seem not to be features of the brain.

For example, my mind experiences QUALIA when I smell a rose or eat a toffee, but it is not clear that my brain has such a conscious experience.

I am infallibly aware of what I am thinking and feeling – if think I'm feeling sad, then I really am feeling sad; I cannot be wrong about it. But I am *not* infallibly aware of which neurones are firing in my brain, or which neurochemicals are being released. So it might seem that the mind and the brain are different from one another.

Furthermore, I have FIRST-PERSON IMMEDIATE ACCESS to my thoughts; they are LOGICALLY PRIVATE to me. If I am remembering a meeting when I spilled a drink, then I am immediately aware of this thought in a way that no one else is. Even if I'm connected to a brain scanner, others might be able to see I'm feeling embarrassed, but they cannot know the exact content of my thoughts in the way I can.

However, all of these proofs rest on Leibniz's Law of identity, and they are unconvincing to physicalists because they may commit the MASKED MAN FALLACY.

Masked man fallacy

All of Descartes' 'proofs' (and indeed all claims which rely on Leibniz's Law) are vulnerable to the MASKED MAN FALLACY, because they assume that the *appearance* of different properties is proof that the two things in question are different entities (for example, that the mind is distinct from the brain).

Leibniz's Law is true: if A is the same thing as B, then A and B will definitely have the same properties. However, it is possible for us to know some properties of A and some properties of B, *without realising* that they are the same thing. Consider this argument:

1. My idea of Batman is a man who wears a mask and fights crime
2. My idea of Bruce Wayne is a man who doesn't wear a mask, and is a superficial billionaire
3. If A is the same thing as B, then whatever is true of A will also be true of B (Leibniz's Law)

C. Therefore, Bruce Wayne is not Batman

It should be clear to anyone who knows about superheroes that this argument is flawed, because Bruce Wayne is in fact Batman. The argument doesn't demonstrate that Batman isn't Bruce Wayne – all it demonstrates is that I don't know the full picture. When Descartes argues analogously to the conclusion that the mind is not the brain, he could be making the same sort of fallacious argument.

Ghost in the machine

Ryle argues that dualism rests on a CATEGORY MISTAKE (see p17); this is when something is placed into the wrong logical category.

Ryle suggests that dualists make a category mistake when they wrongly assume that the mind is more than just the brain. It's as if the dualist sees the neurones firing in the brain, the hormones being released, and the signals being set to the spinal cord, but then asks "But where is the mind?" when in fact the neurones, hormones and signals *are* the mind. Ryle suggests that dualists are looking for 'THE GHOST IN THE MACHINE' when they assume that something supernatural (a mental substance) exists within a purely physical structure.

Strengths

- Cartesian dualism is popular among people who believe in life after death, because it allows that our minds (or souls) can exist after the physical body dies.
- We sometimes talk as if the mind and the body are distinct.
- It seems hard to admit that the experience of falling in love, going on a rollercoaster, and feeling grief-stricken are just neurochemical occurrences; QUALIA seem to be non-physical.

Criticisms

- It is not clear why one mind is associated with one body: one body could have numerous minds (souls) and we wouldn't know it (the PROBLEM OF COUNTING SOULS).
- The mind and body appear to interact (when I feel sad, my eyes start to cry); it seems clear that the mind is linked to the body – perhaps because the mind is the brain.

Response: The mind and body are INTERMINGLED so that I can feel pain rather than just notice injury (see p97). A human is a composite substance consisting of both a mind and a body.

Criticisms

- Many of Descartes' 'proofs' are fallacious or weak arguments because they BEG THE QUESTION, commit the MASKED MAN FALLACY or make a CATEGORY MISTAKE.
- Science is increasingly showing us that particular areas of the brain are responsible for particular thoughts, sensations or abilities; it certainly seems that the mind and brain are the same thing.
- Due to the 'CAUSAL CLOSURE' of the physical universe, something non-physical cannot cause something physical, so if minds are non-physical, then they are CAUSALLY INERT; they cannot cause anything in the physical body (see p110).
- Biology suggests that mindedness is not just a feature of humans, but that animals are conscious to some extent. It is likely that consciousness didn't just appear suddenly in our evolution, but rather, developed and evolved as the brain did. And consciousness doesn't suddenly appear in babies, but develops over a period of months or years, as the brain develops. This all points to the mind not being a separate substance, but a mere feature of the brain.

Also see the strengths and criticisms of the ARGUMENT FROM CONCEIVABILITY (p101), the ARGUMENT FROM INDIVISIBILITY (p105), and the MIND-BODY INTERACTION PROBLEM (p107).

Dualist Argument from Conceivability

Overview

Key philosopher: Descartes

The CARTESIAN DUALIST argument from conceivability is an attempt by Descartes to demonstrate that the mind and brain are different substances. He suggests that because he can conceive of a mind existing without a brain/body, this demonstrates that the mind is not the brain, and the mind is a non-physical substance.

You may recall from your study of Epistemology for Paper 1 that when Descartes has his 'waves of doubt' he considers the idea that he could be being tricked by an evil demon. He realises that he could be a disembodied mind being fooled into thinking he has a body. In imagining this, Descartes conceives of a mind existing without a body. His argument can be summarised as:

1. I can conceive of my mind existing without my brain
2. (implied) Whatever is conceivable is metaphysically possible
3. (implied) Therefore it's metaphysically possible for my mind to exist without my brain
4. (implied) If A is the same thing as B, then whatever is true of A will also be true of B (Leibniz's Law)

C. Therefore, my mind and brain are different substances

Physical and metaphysical possibility

When Descartes says that the mind can be *conceived of* without the body, we must consider what it means for something to be conceivable. By conceivable, Descartes means that it is LOGICALLY POSSIBLE or METAPHYSICALLY POSSIBLE. In other words, we can imagine it happening, even if it couldn't happen in the world as we know it.

Descartes is relying on the assumption that if it were metaphysically impossible for a mind to exist without a body, then we wouldn't be able to conceive of it – in the same way we cannot conceive of a round square.

Criticisms

At first glance, this may seem like a fairly convincing argument, given the truth of Leibniz's Law – however, there are several criticisms of it.

What is conceivable may not be metaphysically possible

Arnauld points out that just because something is conceivable doesn't mean it is metaphysically possible: sometimes, people can conceive of things which are metaphysically impossible. For example, someone who doesn't know Pythagoras' theorem can conceive of a right-angled triangle where the square of the hypotenuse is *not* equal to the squares of the other two sides. Anyone who knows about the theorem will know that this is a metaphysical impossibility, but still some people can conceive of it.

So even though Descartes can conceive of a mind without a body, it could still be metaphysically impossible; it could simply be that Descartes is misunderstanding the nature of the mind in the same way that a person can misunderstand the nature of right-angled triangles.

Masked man fallacy

Descartes commits the MASKED MAN FALLACY (see p17 and 99) with his argument from conceivability. Just because he *conceives of* the mind and the body as having different features, this does not prove that they are indeed different. Lois Lane makes the same mistake when she considers the properties of Superman and Clark Kent and concludes that they're different.

Begging the question

Descartes BEGS THE QUESTION when he suggests with his first premise that one can conceive of the mind without the brain. This is because he assumes that the mind is a different thing from the brain – an assumption which a physicalist would deny.

Physicalist position

A PHYSICALIST would suggest that it is *not* possible to conceive of the mind existing without the brain, because the mind *is* the brain. If Descartes were to suggest that H_2O is conceivable without water, anyone who knows about chemistry would realise that he was making a mistake: H_2O cannot exist without water, because they are the same thing.

Anyone who *can* conceive of H_2O without water is making a mistake; the same may be true of anyone who can conceive of the mind without the brain.

<table>
<tr><td colspan="2">Functionalist response
FUNCTIONALISTS would disagree with the other physicalists here, by suggesting that a mind can be a brain, a computer, an alien ball of slime, or something else entirely – whatever functions as a mind, is a mind. So functionalists can conceive of a mind without a (human) brain.</td></tr>
<tr><td>What would remain of a disembodied mind?
It is difficult to conceive of a mind without a body, because the two are so closely linked (even Descartes admitted that the two are INTERMINGLED – see p97). A disembodied mind could not see anything, because it would have no eyes, and it could not feel any pain, heat or other sensations, because it would have no senses.

Psychologists have found that there are areas of the brain which store our memories, so perhaps the disembodied mind would not have any memories either. It is difficult to understand exactly what would remain when all the physical aspects of the brain and body had been removed. So maybe a mind without a body is not conceivable.</td><td>Response
Functionalists might suggest that it is conceivable for a person to have their memories downloaded into a computer or other machine (see FUNCTIONALISM, above and p137). A mind might need some sort of physical storage device, but that physical device needn't be an organic brain. If a mind could exist artificially, then that is enough to demonstrate that the mind is not the same thing as the brain.</td></tr>
<tr><td>Hard behaviourist position
Hempel's hard behaviourism (see p125) would suggest that a mind without a body is inconceivable, because hard behaviourists view minds in terms of behaviour.

A non-physical disembodied mind cannot behave in any way at all, and without behaviour there is no mind. So a mind without a body is inconceivable.</td><td>Response
Sadly, there are disabilities where the person is unable to move at all, but their mind remains just as active and alert as anybody else's mind; they still have a mind but no behaviour.</td></tr>
</table>

Metaphysical possibility is not actual possibility

Simply because something is metaphysically possible does not prove that it is ACTUALLY POSSIBLE in the real world. Anything that can be imagined is metaphysically possible, such as a baby swimming through the sun, a three-headed donkey-fish, or a rock which sings and dances – yet none of these are *actually* possible. So even if the mind and the body can be conceived of as separate, this does not show that they can exist separately in the actual world.

Conception doesn't prove different substances

Even if we were to admit that we can conceive of the mind without the body, this does not prove that they are different substances; they could still both be physical substances, or the mind might not be a substance at all. Consider these two arguments:

1. I can conceive of a hand existing without bones
2. Whatever is conceivable is metaphysically possible
3. Therefore it's metaphysically possible for my hand to exist without bones
4. If A is the same thing as B, then whatever is true of A will also be true of B (Leibniz's Law)

C. Therefore, hands and bones are different substances

1. I can conceive of time existing without clocks
2. Whatever is conceivable is metaphysically possible
3. Therefore it's metaphysically possible for time to exist without clocks
4. If A is the same thing as B, then whatever is true of A will also be true of B (Leibniz's Law)

C. Therefore, time and clocks are different substances

These arguments are identical to Descartes' argument from conceivability in their LOGICAL FORM, but it's clear that the conclusions are false. Just because we can conceive of two things existing apart from one another doesn't prove that they are different *substances*.

The first argument is false because hands and bones are both physical substances; this may be true of the mind as well as the brain. It may be the case that minds and brains are *both* physical substances, but are not identical to one another. But just as a hand without bones might be significantly different from a hand with bones, so a mind without a brain could be very different from a mind within a brain.

The second argument is false because time is not a substance at all; this may be true about the mind. The mind might be a non-physical property of the brain (see p113). Although clocks and time are related to one another – because clocks track the passage of time – this does not show that time depends upon clocks. Similarly, the mind may be related to the brain without being dependent upon it, but this doesn't prove it is a non-physical substance.

Dualist Argument from Indivisibility

Overview

Key philosopher: Descartes

The CARTESIAN DUALIST argument from indivisibility is an attempt by Descartes to demonstrate that the mind and brain are different substances. He suggests that because the mind is indivisible (it cannot be split into sections) but the brain is divisible, this demonstrates that the mind is not the brain, and the mind is a non-physical substance. His argument can be summarised as:

1. The mind is indivisible whereas the body is divisible
2. (implied) If A is the same thing as B, then whatever is true of A will also be true of B (Leibniz's Law)

C. Therefore, my mind and brain are different substances

Descartes maintains that extension is an essential property of physical objects, and since the brain is a physical object, it is self-evidently divisible. It is possible to cut the brain in half, for example.

The mind, on the other hand, is not divisible because it is non-physical. It would not be possible to divide the mind into sections; there cannot be half a mind. Based on Leibniz's Law of identity, if the brain is divisible and the mind is not divisible, then they cannot be the same thing as each other.

Criticisms

Descartes' argument is an interesting one, and it may seem fairly convincing, given the truth of Leibniz's Law – however, there are several criticisms of it.

Not everything physical is divisible	**Response**
Not everything physical is divisible – for example, physics tells us that there is a smallest subatomic particle which is indivisible. So although it is true to say that a brain is divisible (it can be chopped up, for example) it is not true to say that *all* physical things are divisible. If not all physical things are divisible, then divisibility is not an essential property of the physical things. This means that the mind – like subatomic particles – could be both physical and indivisible.	Descartes doesn't need to show that *all* physical things are divisible, only that brains are divisible whilst minds are not. However, Descartes doesn't demonstrate that the mind is indivisible. Even if no one has ever divided a mind, we can still conceive of dividing a mind (for example, to separate the intellect from the imagination), and by Descartes' own CONCEIVABILITY ARGUMENT, if something can be conceived of then it is METAPHYSICALLY POSSIBLE. This means that it is metaphysically possible to divide a mind.

The mind is divisible	**Response**
Severe epilepsy is sometimes treated via an operation which separates the hemispheres of the brain, resulting in a 'split brain'. After the operation, each hemisphere operates independently of the other and controls one side of the body. Sometimes the two sides do not work together, and each side of the person's body wants to do different things. It is as though the person has two minds. This suggests that the mind is in fact divisible (not just that it's metaphysically possible to divide it, but that it's ACTUALLY POSSIBLE). The fact that this division of the mind occurs at the same time as the two halves of the brain are separated strongly suggests that the mind is the brain.	This 'two minds working against each other' phenomenon only occurs in a few split brain patients. Most have a split brain but a single mind. Nonetheless, it could be said that people with multiple personality disorder have multiple minds – and yet they only have one brain.

Property dualism
PROPERTY DUALISM (see p113) suggests that mental events are non-physical properties of the brain.

A property of something is not usually divisible. For example, a melon has properties such as being yellow and 7°C, but its yellowness and its temperature are not divisible, even though the melon itself *is* divisible. But we would not conclude from this that yellowness is a different *substance* from a melon.

So according to property dualists, the brain can be divisible while the mind (as a property of the brain) is indivisible, without the mind and the brain being different substances.

Masked man fallacy

Descartes commits the MASKED MAN FALLACY (see p17 and 99) with his argument from indivisibility, as he does in his other proofs that mind and body are distinct substances. Simply because it *seems* to Descartes that the mind is indivisible whereas the body is divisible, this does not prove they are indeed that way. It might *seem* that Batman and Bruce Wayne have different properties, but they are in fact the same person.

In the past, scientists thought that atoms were indivisible, but now we know the atom can be divided into smaller parts; perhaps in future science will discover how to divide the mind too.

Begging the question

The argument from indivisibility BEGS THE QUESTION, because it makes an assumption from the outset that an opponent would contest, namely that the mind is distinct from the brain. The argument suggests that the mind is indivisible whereas the brain is divisible, but this argument would not convince a physicalist that the mind and brain are different, because the physicalist maintains that the mind *is* divisible; you could pull it out of someone's head and cut it up into pieces, because the mind is the brain!

Mind-body Interaction

Overview	**Key philosopher:** Descartes

The problem of MIND-BODY INTERACTION is also known as the MIND-BODY PROBLEM. The mind and body appear to interact with one another, and we must explain how this occurs; this is tricky for substance dualists, as they maintain that one is physical and one is non-physical.

Suppose this chain of events occurs:

- My eyes see a pizza.
- My mind has the thought "I want to eat that pizza."
- My hands reach out, pick up the pizza, and put it in my mouth.
- My mind has the thought "Mmm, yummy!"

It certainly *seems* as though my mind and my body are interacting, but if substance dualism is true, then how is this possible? This is the empirical INTERACTION PROBLEM.

Physicalism: no problem	**Substance dualism: problem**
For PHYSICALISTS – and even PROPERTY DUALISTS – explaining this series of events is not difficult. My brain interacts with my body via my central nervous system; one physical system interacts with another physical system and fires electrical impulses in my brain and body. Physicalism has this scientifically-proven explanation, so the mind-body "problem" is not a problem at all for physicalists.	For substance dualists, explaining how my mind and body interact to eat the pizza is a genuine difficulty, because substance dualists must explain how a non-physical substance such as the mind can interact with a physical substance such as the body. The substance dualist must come up with a plausible explanation of how this occurs, or dualism is severely weakened. (The rest of this section is about how substance dualism can explain mind-body interaction.)

Solutions which rely on God

The two main solutions to the mind-body problem which you need to know are INTERACTIONISM and EPIPHENOMENALISM, but it is useful to know other competing theories which attempt to solve the mind-body problem.

Occasionalism

This theory asserts that God serves as the link between my mind and my body. God observes that light has reflected from a pizza onto my retina and that neurones are firing in my brain, so he causes my mind to have an experience of seeing the pizza. My mind decides to eat the pizza, so God causes another set of neurones to fire in my brain, which results in my hand picking up the pizza and putting it in my mouth. God acts as a middle-man for every single mind-body interaction that everyone ever has; it's a lot of work, but he can do it because he is OMNIPOTENT!

Parallelism

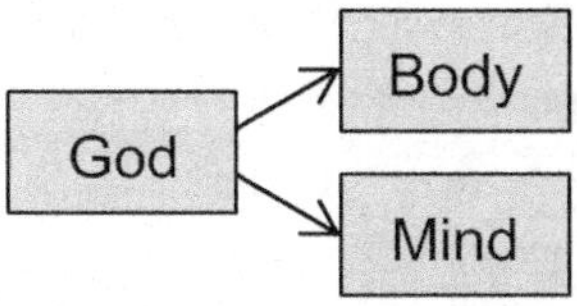

Parallelism asserts that the mind and the body aren't linked at all but simply act in parallel. The mind and the body are constructed (again, by God) so that the events occurring in one are always exactly appropriate to events occurring in the other. Whenever my mind has the thought about wanting to eat a pizza, my brain will tell my hand to reach out and pick up the pizza – but they aren't linked at all, just wonderfully constructed to work in parallel. The mind and the body are like two clocks operating independently, but keeping up with each other so perfectly that it *seems* there is interaction between them.

Are occasionalism and parallelism convincing?

ATHEISTS are of course unconvinced by these explanations of mind-body interaction, as are many religious people. Moreover, it's not PARSIMONIOUS to propose an additional being (God) to solve the mind-body problem if one isn't needed. If we can explain mind-body interaction without reference to God, then we should use OCKHAM'S RAZOR to remove God from the explanation. This is what epiphenomenalism (p111) and interactionism (below) aim to do.

Interactionist dualism

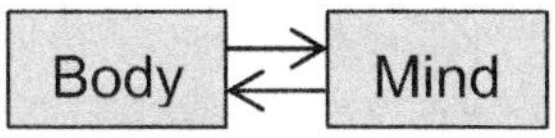

Interactionist dualism answers the mind-body problem by claiming that the mind and body interact with one another, without reference to God. It claims that the mind and body interact with one another directly, which seems far more plausible than the explanations offered by occasionalism or parallelism.

Criticisms

Even though interactionism is an improvement on occasionalism and parallelism, there are still criticisms of it.

Pineal gland is physical

Descartes suggests that the mind and body are INTERMINGLED (see p97), and that they interact with one another through the pineal gland in the brain.

However, science has shown that the primary functions of the pineal gland are to regulate sleep rhythms and to release hormones. Descartes does not believe that animals have minds, and yet pineal glands are present in almost all vertebrates, even very primitive species.

Science has found no evidence that the pineal gland has any connection to higher thoughts or reason. But even if substance dualists continue to maintain that it *does* connect the mind with the brain, they must still explain how a physical pineal gland could interact with a non-physical mind. This means that the pineal gland does not offer any solution at all to the mind-body problem.

Conceptual interaction problem

Princess Elisabeth of Bohemia criticises Descartes' dualism, and she raises the issue of mind-body interaction. She points out that it is not possible for a non-physical mind to make contact with a physical body, and so it seems impossible for the mind to cause movement in the body. Her argument can be summarised as:

1. The body is a physical thing
2. A (physical) thing which moves must have been caused to move by something else physical
3. There must be contact between two things in order for one to move the other
4. According to Descartes, the mind is non-physical
5. It is not possible for a non-physical thing to make contact with a physical thing

C. Therefore, Descartes' account of dualism cannot explain how a non-physical thing can cause movement in a physical thing

Princess Elisabeth suggests that Descartes should admit that the mind is in fact a physical thing, as that would explain MENTAL CAUSATION.

Causal closure of the physical universe

A scientific way to explain Princess Elisabeth's argument is with reference to the CAUSAL CLOSURE OF THE PHYSICAL UNIVERSE. The laws of nature of the physical world tell us that every physical movement or change is always caused by something else physical; there can be no non-physical causes which somehow enter the physical realm and cause physical things to happen. Another way of saying this is that non-physical things are CAUSALLY INERT; they cannot cause anything.

The law of the conservation of energy also tells us that nothing can be given energy (moved) from outside of the physical world. This means that non-physical entities (if they even exist) cannot cause movement in physical entities. The argument can be summarised as:

1. The physical universe is a closed system; energy cannot be created or destroyed (only changed from one form to another)
2. In a closed system, energy is conserved
3. Mind and body causally interact with one another
4. Causation involves the transfer of energy
5. The body is physical

C. Therefore, the mind must be physical

Response

Descartes' response is that mental causation does not occur in the same way as physical causation does. He gives the example of a heavy object falling to Earth because of its weight, but it is not that 'weight' has come into contact with the heavy object and pushed it down. Similarly, mind-body interaction can occur without contact ever being made between the two entities.

This is not a convincing response, and the mind-body problem remains.

Epiphenomenalist Dualism

Overview

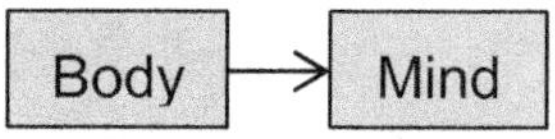

Epiphenomenalism (or epiphenomenalist dualism) is a response to the MIND-BODY PROBLEM for SUBSTANCE DUALISM. It suggests that the body/brain affects the mind, but the mind has no effect on the body/brain. Mental events are mere 'epiphenomena' (by-products of brain activity which cannot cause or affect anything.)

When I see a pizza and I have the thought that I want to eat it, and then I *do* eat it, it might *appear* that the thought in my mind has caused me to eat the pizza, but in fact it has not, according to epiphenomenalism.

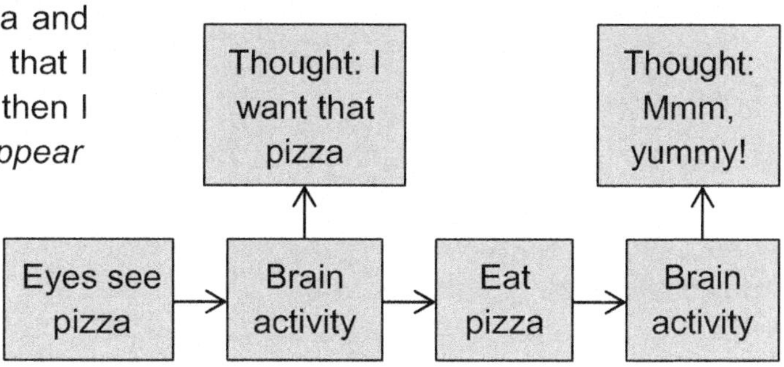

Instead, my sight of the pizza has caused brain activity, which in turn has caused my mind activity (thoughts / desires). But it is my brain activity – *not* the thought in my mind – which causes my hand to reach out and pick up the pizza. My thoughts are CAUSALLY INERT – they do not cause anything in my body.

This means that the chain of events which caused me to eat the pizza is entirely physical, and the thought I had did not cause anything physical.

Strengths	Criticisms
• Epiphenomenalist dualism doesn't rely on anything supernatural such as God, like OCCASIONALISM and PARALLELISM do, so it is more PARSIMONIOUS than they are. • It doesn't claim that something non-physical can affect something physical (however it does suggest that something physical can affect something non-physical!), so it *partially* avoids the 'CAUSAL CLOSURE OF THE PHYSICAL UNIVERSE' criticism of interactionism. • Some scientific studies suggest that some brain-damaged people are able to carry out complex actions when they have no consciousness; this shows that consciousness is not a causal or essential part of our bodily actions. • Critics suggest that epiphenom-enalism is counter-intuitive, but that does not mean it is obviously false; some theories are counter-intuitive and true.	• According to OCKHAM'S RAZOR, causally inert parts of a chain of events can be removed without affecting the outcome, so it seems that mind activities can be removed from epiphenom-enalism, and the chain of events between the brain and the body would remain intact. The mental events are CAUSALLY REDUNDANT – however, without them, it would no longer look like a dualist theory, but a physicalist one. • It is unclear why human brains would evolve to have epiphenomenal thoughts when they are causally redundant. Generally, useless features of animals disappear over time via natural selection (or never develop in the first place): why would humans evolve to have minds which don't affect our behaviour? • Explaining behaviour physically but still retaining the claim that mental states are non-physical seems unsatisfactory; it means we could be ZOMBIES and it wouldn't make any difference.

Criticisms

- The law of the conservation of energy states that all energy in the universe is 'contained' because the universe is a closed system – so when a physical thing such as the brain affects the mind, it would still lose energy, which defies the laws of physics.
- I have introspective self-knowledge (I know my own thoughts), and these thoughts can cause me to take action (e.g. as I reason through an argument or write a story). This ARGUMENT FROM INTROSPECTION suggests that epiphenomenalism is incorrect. Any beliefs I hold cannot have been caused by my mind, as my mind is causally inert. The fact that I can realise a belief by mere introspection suggests that epiphenomenalism is false.
- Princess Elisabeth's argument against dualism (see p110) applies to epiphenomenalism: how can a physical thing affect or come into contact with a non-physical thing?
- The PHENOMENOLOGY of our mental lives (our experience of QUALIA) can have an effect on our (bodily) actions. The denial that our minds can affect our bodies seems counter-intuitive; it seems SELF-EVIDENT that the mind *does* affect the body.
- If I do something bad such as killing, the epiphenomenalist would struggle to blame me for my actions, because he'd first have to show that I chose to act in such a way – but if my mind can't affect my behaviour, then surely I have not *chosen* to kill anyone. Epiphenomenalism seems to remove FREE WILL and responsibility, which we value highly.

Property Dualism

Overview

Key philosopher: Chalmers

Property dualism is an approach which suggests that mental events are non-physical properties of a physical substance – namely, the brain. Property dualists do not claim that there are two types of substance in the universe – in fact, property dualists are MONISTS – but they claim that QUALIA are not reducible to physical events in the brain, so property dualism is a form of NON-REDUCTIVE MONISM.

Physical properties	**Physical and mental properties**
Inanimate objects such as tables, houses and stars only have physical properties.	The brain is a physical entity which can have mental properties. These exist in humans and some animals.

Consciousness is not reducible

We can explain many phenomena scientifically and objectively. For example, colour can be explained in terms of (and thus reduced to) statements about electromagnetic wavelengths; heat can be explained in terms of (and thus reduced to) statements about molecular energy.

According to property dualists, consciousness cannot be explained in terms of (or reduced to) scientific statements, because the *experience* of consciousness *is* the reality; it is INEFFABLE. At least some mental properties are not reducible to physical properties. In other words, property dualists claim that qualia cannot be fully explained in terms of physical brain states; there is something more to them.

Denial of supervenience

Some PHYSICALISTS argue that mental events SUPERVENE on the physical events in the brain, meaning that any change in mental events must have a corresponding change in the brain.

But property dualists deny supervenience. They suggest that at least some mental properties are not supervenient upon physical properties. This means that there can be a change in mental events or properties without a corresponding change in the brain.

Zombie world	**How zombies act**
Chalmers puts forward a thought experiment designed to support property dualism. He maintains that it is possible for there to be a world which is physically identical to ours, (right down to subatomic particles) and the people in such a world would behave exactly as we do, but they are ZOMBIES without any qualia.	It would not be possible to tell the difference between a zombie and a person with qualia, because they would appear exactly the same as us. Their behaviour and brain-waves would be the same as ours; they'd talk, eat, and cry out in pain… but there would be no subjective feelings (i.e. qualia) associated with any of the zombie's experiences.

Zombies in this sense (sometimes referred to as 'philosophical zombies') does not mean re-animated mummies or the undead, it simply means a person who *appears* to have a mind, but in fact does not (see the PROBLEM OF OTHER MINDS, p119).

Chalmers' 'zombie' thought experiment suggests that qualia are something additional to physical brain activity, and cannot be reduced to it. If this is a possibility, then physicalism is false. The zombie argument can be summarised as:

1. It is conceivable that zombies exist
2. Therefore it is metaphysically possible for zombies to exist
3. If it is metaphysically possible that zombies exist, then mental events are non-physical

C. Therefore, property dualism is true

Strengths

- The zombie world does seem conceivable and metaphysically possible, and so qualia cannot be wholly physical.
- Qualia do seem to be more than just neurochemical reactions in brains; they have an INEFFABLE quality which perhaps cannot be explained in physical terms alone; they are a special property of the brain.

Criticisms

- We don't fully understand consciousness yet. A physicalist might suggest that when we more fully understand qualia, we'll realise that qualia can be wholly explained in terms of brain states, so a zombie is an impossibility.

Criticisms

- A zombie world may not be conceivable – if we *think* we can conceive of a zombie with a functioning brain but no qualia, then we are making a mistake with our reasoning, in the same way that someone may claim they can conceive of a round square.
- Even if a zombie world is conceivable, it may not be metaphysically possible; we can sometimes conceive of things which are metaphysically impossible, such as a triangle whose internal angles do not add up to 180°.
- Thought experiments don't always tell us about reality: even if a zombie world *is* metaphysically possible, this does not demonstrate that property dualism is *true*; it just shows that property dualism is *possible* – so the conclusion is not entailed by the premises.

Criticisms

- The zombie argument BEGS THE QUESTION: it assumes that there can exist a zombie with identical brain activity to me but lacking a mind, but if physicalism is true then such a thought experiment cannot be possible. Property dualism seems to assume that a functional brain can lack qualia, which is the very point it is trying to prove.
- If zombies can exist, then property dualism is not the only possibility. SUBSTANCE DUALISM could be a conclusion drawn from the zombie argument; the people are zombies because they lack a mental substance.

Mary's Black and White Room

Overview | **Key philosopher:** Jackson

Mary's black and white room (also known as 'Mary the super-scientist' or the 'knowledge/Mary argument for property dualism') is a thought experiment by Jackson which is intended to support PROPERTY DUALISM. The thought experiment can be summarised as:

Mary has been kept in a black and white room since birth; she has always worn a suit which covers her entire body, so she has never seen her skin or hair. This means she has never seen colour in her life. She has been highly educated though, and she lives in the future at a time when neuroscience has a complete understanding of the brain, the eyes, and so on.

She is a specialist in human vision and knows everything about the physics and physiology of colour perception. She knows exactly what occurs in the eyes and brain when a human being sees colours, yet she has never seen a colour. One day Mary escapes from her monochromatic room, and comes out into the real world where she sees colour for the first time.

When Mary sees colour for the first time, does she learn anything new? Jackson argues that Mary will learn something new: she'll learn what it is *like* to see colour (she'll have the QUALIA of colour vision).

It is said that qualia are INTROSPECTIVELY ACCESSIBLE and SUBJECTIVE, meaning that one can only know what an experience is like by experiencing it for themselves.

I can understand echolocation, but I cannot know what it is *like* to be a bat using echolocation. Qualia are also said to be INTRINSIC or non-representational properties of mental states, meaning that qualia can only be *experienced*; they cannot be understood by examining the brain.

Jackson argues that even though Mary knew all the facts about colour vision, she had not experienced the qualia, so didn't know what it was *like* to see colour until she saw it. Jackson's argument can be summarised as:

1. Mary knew every physical fact about colour vision and neurology
2. Mary experienced something new when she saw colours for the first time (the qualia of colour vision)
3. Therefore knowing all the physical facts does not provide a complete account of colour vision

C. Therefore, physicalism is false

Physicalism maintains that mental experiences are nothing more than the physical facts about the brain, but Mary knew all the physical facts, yet she still did not know what it was *like* to see colour; a supposedly non-physical fact. Knowing the physical facts about the brain cannot tell you what it feels like to have a particular experience. This suggests that PHENOMENAL properties (qualia) cannot be understood by knowing the physical facts alone, which means physicalism is false.

Responses to the Mary thought experiment

Jackson's thought experiment about Mary may seem convincing, however there are several criticisms of it:

Acquaintance / ability knowledge	**Response**
Paul Churchland suggests that Mary does not gain any additional PROPOSITIONAL KNOWLEDGE (facts about colour), but she does gain ACQUAINTANCE KNOWLEDGE (familiarity with colour). Lewis argues similarly, that Mary gains no new propositional knowledge, but she does gain new ABILITY KNOWLEDGE. For example, she learns how to distinguish red from blue, how to imagine yellow, and how to recognise green.	Propositional knowledge, ability knowledge and acquaintance knowledge are all linked. For example, in becoming acquainted with red, Mary learns the propositional fact that 'red looks like this'. From that propositional knowledge, she gains the ability to recognise red when she sees it.

No new knowledge	**Response**
A physicalist might suggest that if Mary really *does* know all the physical facts about seeing colour, then she understands the PHENOMENOLOGY of colour vision. This means that she doesn't learn anything new when she sees colours for the first time, because all physical knowledge includes knowledge of qualia.	This response is COUNTER-INTUITIVE because, as Hume's empiricism suggests, it doesn't seem possible for someone to work out what it is *like* to see colour without ever having experienced it.
New knowledge, old fact	**Response**
There may be more than one way of knowing the same fact. A person may know that he likes vinegar on his chips, but suppose one day, someone gives him chips with acetic acid solution on them, and he discovers he likes these chips too. He hasn't really learnt anything new, (because vinegar *is* acetic acid solution). Mary had the theoretical concept of red while she was in the black and white room, but when she left the room she gained the PHENOMENAL concept of red (the experience), even though the phenomenal concept and the theoretical concept of red are in fact the same thing. Mary does not gain knowledge of a new property, but she can describe her experiences in a new way, with reference to colours.	It still seems as though Mary *does* gain something when she sees colour for the first time, in the same way that a person gains new knowledge when they discover that vinegar is acetic acid solution. Mary also learns to attribute the new experience to the physical knowledge she already possessed. Similarly, someone can describe an experience to you, but it is different from experiencing it yourself.
Non-existent qualia	**Response**
Paul Churchland and Patricia Churchland put forward the ELIMINATIVIST argument that qualia do not actually exist. Talking about qualia is merely an old-fashioned FOLK PSYCHOLOGICAL way of talking about mental states, and when neuroscience makes further advances, we should (and	It seems counter-intuitive to suggest that qualia don't exist. I know that I have unique experiences which have a particular feel to them. It's presumptuous for Dennett and the

will) abandon talk of qualia, and only talk of neurochemical states instead. Similarly, Dennett argues that qualia do not exist, and when we describe a quale, there is nothing subjective which the description refers to (see p133-134).	Churchlands to try to tell people that they aren't having the experiences they think they are.

The Problem of Other Minds

<table>
<tr><td colspan="2">Overview</td><td>Key philosophers: Mill, Wittgenstein</td></tr>
<tr><td colspan="3">The problem of other minds addresses the question of whether other people have minds; this is primarily a problem for DUALISM.

I can see other people walking around, talking, and behaving like they have minds – but do they? How can I be certain?</td></tr>
<tr><td colspan="3">Who is this a problem for?</td></tr>
<tr><td>For IDENTITY THEORISTS and ELIMINATIVE MATERIALISTS, this is not really a problem: the mind is the brain, therefore if other people have brains, they have minds.</td><td>For FUNCTIONALISTS and BEHAVIOURISTS, this is not really a problem: other people function / behave as though they have minds, therefore they have minds.</td><td rowspan="2">For dualists, who suggest that the mind is a NON-PHYSICAL SUBSTANCE or property, the problem of other minds is a genuine problom, as it is not easy to tell whether other people have properties or non-physical substances.</td></tr>
<tr><td colspan="2">A criticism of the physicalist theories is that it is metaphysically possible for a person to have a brain, and to behave like they have a mind, when in fact they don't – they are a ZOMBIE (see p114). However, physicalism denies the possibility of zombies, so the 'problem' of other minds is not a problem for physicalism.</td></tr>
<tr><td colspan="3">Ryle argues that the problem of other minds is a flaw of dualism. This is because dualism portrays the mind as something totally private and inaccessible to others, meaning that we cannot be sure whether others have minds at all, and any discussion of them is problematic.</td></tr>
</table>

Solipsism

SOLIPSISM is the notion that I am the only minded being in existence. This would be the case if the other people I see walking and talking are ZOMBIES, i.e. although they *appear* to have minds, they are mindless.

You may recall from your study of idealism for Paper 1 that solipsism is not a philosophically strong stance to take, so the problem of other minds must be solved if dualism is to redeem itself.

Wittgenstein's beetle

Wittgenstein puts forward a thought experiment in order to demonstrate the absurdity of talking about minds with other people (see left panel).

Suppose everyone has a box, with something in it which they call a 'beetle'. No one can look in anyone else's box. A person says he knows what a beetle is simply by looking in his own box.	Wittgenstein points out that the problem with the beetle in the box is that everyone could have something totally different in his or her box, and no one would realise. It is possible that some people have nothing at all in their boxes, and are just saying they have a beetle. So beetles cannot be meaningfully discussed, as I cannot be sure whether other people have beetles, or whether their beetles are like mine. The same is true of minds.

Private language

Wittgenstein answers his own 'beetle' argument and tries to refute solipsism by pointing out that if I was the only minded creature in existence, then I would not be able to construct a language. Given that I converse in a language, this suggests that the language has not been created by me alone, and that other people are language users with minds too. The reason I can meaningfully use terms such as 'blue', 'pain' and 'sadness' is because others have these same sensations and thus the words have a shared meaning among language users.

Criticisms of Wittgenstein

- It may be possible for someone to construct a private language, and Wittgenstein cannot demonstrate that this is impossible.
- Even if language *is* shared with others, this does not prove that other people have minds. A child could only interact with a talking toy, and thus he could learn language, but the toy is nonetheless mindless.
- It's possible that *some* people have minds and others are zombies.

Argument from analogy

Mill's argument from analogy is a response to the problem of other minds.

Me	I stub my toe	→	Mental state: pain	→	Pain behaviour (shouting, swearing, holding my foot)
Other person	He stubs his toe	→	?	→	Pain behaviour (shouting, swearing, holding his foot)

Mill notes that although we can't observe other people's inner mind states, we can observe their behaviour, and things that trigger their behaviour. For example, in my own case, I know that when I stub my toe, this causes my inner mind state of pain, and this in turn causes me to shout, swear, and hold my foot. In other people, I see the same trigger and their same response, and I can reason by analogy from my own case that they probably experience the inner mind state of pain just as I do. This argument can be summarised as:

1. I know that in my own case, particular events cause particular mental states, which cause me to behave in particular ways
2. In others, I observe these same events, followed by their behaving in ways similar to my own
3. Other people have bodies like mine
4. Other people display behaviour like mine
5. I have a mind

C. Therefore, other people have minds like mine

The argument from analogy uses ABDUCTIVE REASONING to make an INFERENCE TO THE BEST EXPLANATION; this means that although it does not prove the existence of other people's minds with certainty, other people having minds is a better explanation for their behaviour than a zombie world is.

Strength	**Criticisms**
• The argument from analogy – and other people having minds – is the best explanation for other people's behaviour.	• The argument from analogy only shows that other people *behave* like they're in pain – but a SUPER-SPARTAN can be in pain but not show it, and an actor can show pain when there is none. **Response**: Actors and Spartans can do this because they have minds

Criticisms

- How similar does other people's behaviour need to be? If I see someone stub their toe and just carry on walking, do I conclude that they don't have a mind?
- It is possible that the stubbed toe causes the pain behaviour directly, *not* that the pain causes the pain behaviour.

Stubbed toe	→	Pain behaviour
	→	Pain

OCKHAM'S RAZOR tells us that the 'pain' element can be removed in others, and the pain behaviour could remain.

- Ryle argues that there is no possible way to ever VERIFY or FALSIFY the claim that others' minds are like my own, so the argument is flawed (see p81 and 87).
- Generalising from one case (my own) to all other cases is a weak form of reasoning.

Response: It is usually a flawed idea to generalise from one case to many, but in this instance there is no other data I could study; my own case is all the information I have available.

- Other people acting similarly to me is not proof; noticing similarities does not allow us to logically infer other unseen similarities.

Response: The argument is not attempting to logically *prove* the existence of other minds; only to offer the best explanation for the behaviour of other people.

Best hypothesis argument

This ABDUCTIVE ARGUMENT attempts to respond to the problem of other minds by outlining two competing hypotheses, and suggesting that other people having minds is the best one.

Other people walk, talk, cry, laugh, act as if they are in pain, and say that they have subjective, PHENOMENAL experiences. Given these behaviours, there are (at least) two hypotheses which can explain what's going on. The hypotheses are:

(a) other people have minds roughly similar to mine

(b) other people are mindless zombies

Like the argument from analogy, the argument to the best hypothesis accepts that we cannot be INFALLIBLY certain about the existence of other minds. However, given these two competing hypotheses, (a) is the best explanation of the facts.

Does dualism survive the problem of other minds?

Although the argument from analogy and the best hypothesis argument have far more criticisms than strengths, this is perhaps an occasion where a single strength outweighs all the criticisms.

If the argument from analogy or the best hypothesis argument are convincing enough, then dualism can survive the problem of other minds. However if we are unconvinced by the arguments (for example, if we demand *certainty* that other people have minds) then dualism can slip into solipsism, and this is a serious problem for dualists.

Physicalism

Overview

Physicalism is a MATERIALIST theory, as it suggests that everything is made up of physical matter (elements, atoms, quarks etc) and there is no such thing as a mental substance. Thus, it is a MONIST theory, as physicalists maintain that there is only one substance in the universe.

Physicalists suggest that everything is physical or SUPERVENES on the physical. There are four physicalist theories you need to know (note that functionalism is not *always* characterised as a physicalist theory):

Behaviourism This theory suggests that mindedness is simply behaviour. This includes HARD BEHAVIOURISM and SOFT BEHAVIOURISM.	**Identity theory** This theory suggests that mental states are identical to (can be ONTOLOGICALLY REDUCED to) brain states. This includes TOKEN IDENTITY THEORY and TYPE IDENTITY THEORY.
Functionalism This theory suggests that if something performs the function of a mind, then it *is* a mind; the mind can be MULTIPLY REALISED.	**Eliminative materialism** This theory suggests that there are no QUALIA or mental states, and terms relating to mental states should be eliminated from our language.

The physicalist theories all have some features in common – in particular, behaviourism and functionalism share some similarities, and identity theory and eliminative materialism also share some similarities.

This means that there is some overlap in the criticisms (and strengths) of these theories. Some general strengths and criticisms of physicalist theories are given below.

Strengths	Criticisms
• The theory of relativity states that space and time form a single continuum; anything which exists in time also exists in space. Mental events exist in time, so must also exist in space, and so they must be physical in their nature. • Physicalism is PARSIMONIOUS because it does not posit a an elusive mental substance which could be called the 'GHOST IN THE MACHINE'. • It does not have to face the MIND-BODY PROBLEM and explain how non-physical minds inexplicably manage to interact with physical bodies. • Physicalism fits in with neuroscience and psychology which tell us that parts of the brain perform different mental functions.	• We still often have the sense that the mind is something more than just the brain; the feelings of qualia do not appear to be merely physical occurrences. • Science has not been able to explain all PHENOMENOLOGICAL events or consciousness – perhaps these things are unexplainable by science because they occur within a non-physical mental substance which cannot be studied scientifically. Also see the strengths and criticisms of BEHAVIOURISM (below), IDENTITY THEORY (p129), ELIMINATIVE MATERIALISM (p133), and FUNCTIONALISM (p137).

Behaviourism

Overview	**Key philosophers:** Ryle, Hempel, Vienna Circle

Behaviourism is a PHYSICALIST theory of mind, as it suggests that everything is physical or SUPERVENES on the physical; there is not a separate mental substance. It is an approach which focuses on the behaviour of a being (such as a human or animal), suggesting that MINDEDNESS simply *is* behaviour.

Philosophical behaviourism

Philosophical behaviourism is an umbrella term, which includes HARD BEHAVIOURISM and SOFT BEHAVIOURISM.

Hard behaviourism	Soft behaviourism
Put forward by Hempel, hard behaviourism suggests that all descriptions of mental states can be reduced without loss of meaning into descriptions of behaviour, using the language of physics to describe bodily movements or states.	Put forward by Ryle, soft behaviourism suggests that all descriptions of mental states are descriptions of behavioural dispositions, using ordinary language.

Logical positivism and hard behaviourism

You may recall the LOGICAL POSITIVISTS from the Moral Philosophy and Metaphysics of God modules. Logical positivists such as Hempel (who was in the VIENNA CIRCLE), suggest that a statement is only factually meaningful if it is either ANALYTIC or VERIFIABLE (in principle) (see p81).

A statement such as "Jack is hopeful" is not analytic, as it is not true by definition, so in order for it to be meaningful it must be verifiable. To verify its truth, we would look to see Jack's behaviour, such as whether he is crossing his fingers, saying "please, come on", and so on.

Behaviourists suggest that there is no way to verify whether Jack is hopeful other than checking his behaviour (asking him if he's feeling hopeful and getting the answer 'yes' is just another form of behaviour). Even a brain scan would not show us whether Jack is feeling hopeful. So for the logical positivists, talk of mental states must either be meaningless, or reducible to verifiable behaviour. This is known as HARD BEHAVIOURISM.

Analytic reductions

When hard behaviourists say that all propositions about minds can be reduced to propositions about behaviour, this is an ANALYTIC REDUCTION, because it suggests that we can replace talk about the mental with talk about behaviour. Thus hard behaviourism is sometimes known as ANALYTIC BEHAVIOURISM.

The language of physics

Hard behaviourists argue that talk of mental states can be reduced (without loss of meaning) to talk of behaviour, using the language of physics. So the statement "Zach is feeling stressed out" (a statement about a mental state) can perhaps be reduced to "Zach's body has cortisol and adrenaline surging through it, his heartbeat is racing, and he is biting his fingernails" (a statement about behaviour).

Category mistake

A hard behaviourist might claim that other theories of mind such as DUALISM and even IDENTITY THEORY rest on a CATEGORY MISTAKE (see p17).

For example, if someone says "I know I've seen her behaviour, but where is her mind?" this is a category mistake according to hard behaviourists because there is nothing more to someone's mind than their behaviour. This is the same type of mistake which a tourist makes when he says "I know I've seen all the colleges and libraries in Oxford, but where is the university?" Oxford University *is* the colleges and libraries, just as the mind *is* behaviour.

Multiple realisability

MULTIPLE REALISABILITY is the notion that a single mental state can manifest itself in a number of different ways. With hard behaviourism, the concern is that a single mental state – for example, 'hoping it snows tomorrow' might have various associated behaviours, including checking the weather, buying a sledge, staring into space, talking about snow, and so on.

Furthermore, a behaviour such as looking at a child might be correlated with various different mental states, such as wishing for a child, being glad one doesn't have a child, thinking that children are silly, remembering being a child, and so on.

Multiple realisability is a genuine problem for hard behaviourism, because someone's behaviour doesn't tell the full story about their inner mental states (even asking someone what they are thinking about might not yield the truth).

Actors and super-Spartans

Putnam suggests that the super-Spartans can behave as if they feel no pain, when in fact they *are* in pain, and an actor can *appear* to be in pain when he is not really. Thus the hard behaviourist claim that a mental state is reducible to behaviour seems implausible.

Soft behaviourism

Ryle's SOFT BEHAVIOURISM is better able to cope with the problems of multiple realisability and actors and the super-Spartans. Soft behaviourism accepts that there is something more to a mental state than mere behaviour.

Dispositions

Ryle uses the notion of DISPOSITIONS to explain the times when someone's behaviour does not seem to correlate with their mental state. Having a disposition is like having a tendency: a glass window is *disposed* to shatter, even if it is never shattered.

To be in pain is to be *disposed* to showing pain behaviour (shouting, crying, holding the sore part of the body, etc). When Mike is in pain, he has the *disposition* to display pain behaviour, even if he does not display any such behaviour.

Strengths

- Soft behaviourism accepts that inner mental states do exist in the form of dispositions.
- Many mental states (e.g. pain, sadness) have corresponding behaviours.
- Behaviour is observable and VERIFIABLE in a way that mental states are not, so it's easier to study behaviour than mental states.
- We generally do infer others' mental states from observing their behaviour.
- Soft behaviourism can account for the multiple realisability of mental states.
- Behaviourism does not struggle with the PROBLEM OF OTHER MINDS: other people *behave* like they have minds, therefore they have minds.
- Behaviourism does not have to explain MIND-BODY INTERACTION, since it only suggests the existence of one substance; the physical.
- According to Wittgenstein, mental states must refer to behaviours, because if they only referred to private internal states, then we wouldn't be able to discuss them with other people (see p120).

Criticisms

- Mental states can be shown in various ways: fear behaviours might be crying, screaming, running, or other behaviours (multiple realisability). Similarly, one behaviour (e.g. staring into space) may be related to any number of mental states, such as hoping, recalling, or knowing; hard behaviourism cannot account for this.
- Sadly, there are conditions such as 'locked in syndrome' where the person is unable to move at all, but their mind remains as active and alert as everyone else's. The person has mental states, but no behaviour.
- Hard behaviourism cannot explain why people behave in particular ways. Physics can tell us why snooker balls move the way they do, but it is difficult or impossible to explain human behaviour without reference to mental states.
- There's an asymmetry between self-knowledge and my knowledge of others' mental states: I easily know when I am in pain, but I have to infer when others are in pain based on their behaviour. This suggests that there is an inner mental experience which is not reducible to behaviour, so hard behaviourism fails.
- Putnam points out that people such as the 'super-Spartans' can feel pain but display no pain behaviour. Similarly, actors can display pain behaviour but not feel any pain.

Response: Soft behaviourism suggests that the super-Spartans are *disposed* to display pain behaviour, even if they don't actually show it.

- SUBSTANCE DUALISTS suggest that we can conceive of a mind without any related behaviour, e.g. a mind/soul after the death of the body could still have emotions or memories.
- There is a danger of circularity when behaviourists claim a particular behaviour occurs because of other behaviours; it seems more likely that behaviour occurs because of inner mind states.
- Dualists suggest that although behaviour is physical and can be explained in terms of physics, the mind is another substance entirely.
- A moment of INTROSPECTION will show me that there is more to me than just behaviour; I am aware of my own mind and my mind cannot be explained in terms of behaviour, so hard behaviourism fails.

Identity theory

Overview

Key philosopher: Smart

Identity theory is a PHYSICALIST theory of mind, as it suggests that everything is physical or SUPERVENES on the physical; there is not a separate mental substance. It is an approach which suggests that mental states are identical to brain states. It is not that our brain states *cause* our mind states; rather, our brain states *are* our mind states.

Neuroscience and psychology are increasingly demonstrating that areas of the brain are responsible for particular functions such as memory, language, spatial awareness, and mathematics. Damage to a particular region of the brain can have pronounced effects in a person's ability to reason, remember, or perform practical tasks. Identity theorists explain this by pointing out that the mind *is* the brain.

Ontological reduction

Identity theorists such as Smart maintain that all mental states are identical to brain states; this is an ONTOLOGICAL REDUCTION, meaning that mental states and brain states are in fact the same thing. Identity theorists claim that all talk of mind states can be reduced to talk of brain processes (pain simply *is* the firing of particular neurones; happiness simply *is* the release of particular chemicals).

However, it is not an ANALYTIC REDUCTION, because we use the terms 'mental state' and 'brain state' to mean different things; they are not synonymous. Nor is 'pain is the firing of nociceptors' meant to be ANALYTICALLY TRUE in the same way that 'triangles have three sides' is analytically true; it's just that the terms 'pain' and 'the firing of nociceptors' refer to the same thing.

Water is identical to H_2O, but we don't use the terms 'water' and 'H_2O' to mean the same thing; when we are talking about drinks or baths we say 'water', whereas when we are in a chemistry class we call it 'H_2O'. So water is ontologically reducible to H_2O but not analytically reducible. The same is true of mental states and brain states, or the mind and the brain; they refer to the same thing, but we use the terms differently.

Types and tokens

The terms 'identical' or 'the same' can have different meanings, so philosophers distinguish NUMERICAL IDENTITY from QUALITATIVE IDENTITY. Above there are three smiley faces which are qualitatively identical (they're the same colour, size etc) but numerically different – because there are three of them; not just one. In other words, the smiley faces are all the same TYPE, but different TOKENS.

Mind-brain type identity theory (MB-type-IT)	Mind-brain token identity theory (MB-token-IT)
This theory suggests that a general type of mind state can be matched exactly to a particular brain state. For example, every time anyone thinks about the ocean, they will have the same brain state.	This theory suggests that each token mind state can be matched exactly to a particular brain state. For example, my thought about the ocean today matches a particular brain state, whereas your thought about the ocean yesterday matched a different (but probably similar) brain state. This theory is also called ANOMALOUS MONISM.

MB-type-IT is open to the criticism of MULTIPLE REALISABILITY, because if it turns out that my brain state when I think about the ocean is different from your brain state when you think about the ocean – or that my brain state today is different from mine tomorrow (when thinking about the ocean) – then the theory is implausible.

MB-token-IT solves the problem of multiple realisability, but we may struggle to draw any conclusions about how a mental state and a brain state correspond to one another at all. If 100 people all do the same calculation, and all of them have different neuroreceptors firing and different chemicals being released, then just how can we say that a particular brain state is identical to a particular mind state? There is no identicalness.

Parsimony

Smart argues that identity theory is more PARSIMONIOUS than dualism because it doesn't propose the existence of mystical non-physical minds. Neuroscience supports much of identity theory, and identity theorists argue that as science progresses, we will be able to map more mental states to brain states, and see that the mind is nothing above and beyond the brain.

Putnam's argument from conceivability

Putnam gives an argument from conceivability against identity theory. His argument can be summarised as:

1. It is conceivable for a being to have a very different physical constitution from humans', but to have the same thoughts and sensations
2. It is inconceivable (and therefore impossible) for something to both have and not have a particular property

C. Therefore, mental properties cannot be the same as physical properties

Putnam's argument is convincing because it does seem possible to imagine an alien which does not have a brain anything like ours, and yet it can talk, remember, hope, imagine, and have all the mental states which we can experience. If this is possible, then a mind cannot be identical to a (human or other Earth animal's) brain. Because of this sort of argument, it might be more realistic to define a mind in terms of its functions (see p137).

Strengths

- The MASKED MAN FALLACY is not a problem for identity theory: although we use the terms 'mind' and 'brain' differently, they actually refer to the same thing.
- Identity theory has no problem explaining MIND-BODY INTERACTION, as it is done via chemicals in the brain and the central nervous system. It is simply one physical system causing a reaction in another physical system.
- Identity theory is more PARSIMONIOUS than dualism – it doesn't propose additional non-physical entities which aren't needed.
- It is supported by neuroscience, which shows that particular areas of the brain perform particular mental functions.
- MULTIPLE REALISABILITY is not a problem for MB-token-IT because each token of a mental state correlates to its own brain state.

Criticisms

- Multiple realisability is a problem for MB-type-IT, because my brain state of sadness today will be different from my brain state of sadness tomorrow, and possibly very different from my brain state of sadness in 30 years time, so MB-type-IT fails.

Response: MB-token-IT solves this problem by stating that 'sadness' can be realised in multiple different ways within my brain

Criticisms

- Putnam criticises MB-type-IT by arguing that it is possible for a animals to have mental states similar to our own, but with very different brains. If mental states are multiply realisable then they cannot be identical to human brain states (the same may be true for an alien or a robot).
- We talk about minds and brains as if they are different, (we say "brain scanner", "brain damage", and "mind control" – but never "mind scanner", "mind damage" or "brain control"). This shows that we conceive of them as being different.

Response: Mind states are ontologically reducible to brain states, but not analytically reducible – we use the two terms differently even though they refer to the same thing (like the way we use 'water' and H_2O differently).

- We are aware of our own thoughts from a young age, but unaware of our neurones firing; we can observe others' neurones firing via brain scans, but we can't feel their QUALIA. This suggests that the mind states are not identical to brain states.
- MB-token-IT struggles to draw any general conclusions about which brain state correlates with which mental state, because there may be millions of 'sad' brain states.
- Dualists would criticise identity theory using LEIBNIZ'S LAW, e.g. the ARGUMENT FROM DIVISIBILITY or the claim that the brain is physical whereas the mind is non-physical.

Response: These dualist arguments BEG THE QUESTION by assuming that the mind is something other than the brain.

- THE LOCATION PROBLEM: brains and neuroreceptors have spatial locations but thoughts and emotions do not. How can something physical be identical to something non-physical?
- Descartes argues that it's possible to conceive of the mind without the brain, which shows it's METAPHYSICALLY POSSIBLE for one to exist without the other (the CONCEIVABILITY ARGUMENT).

Response: I can conceive of Batman without Bruce Wayne (the MASKED MAN FALLACY); just because something is conceivable doesn't prove it's possible to separate them.

- I have INFALLIBLE, IMMEDIATE ACCESS to my mental states but not to my brain states; if I look at my brain scan, I learn something new about my brain that I didn't already know, suggesting that my mind is not my brain.

Eliminative Materialism

Overview	**Key philosophers:** Churchland(s), Dennett

Eliminative materialism – or eliminativism – is a PHYSICALIST theory of mind, as it suggests that everything is physical or SUPERVENES on the physical; there is not a separate mental substance. It is an approach which claims that when we talk of the mind, we mean the brain, but there are no mental properties or QUALIA. There is nothing that corresponds to mental terms such as 'belief', 'hope', 'thought' and so on.

Reductionism	**Eliminativism**
IDENTITY THEORISTS are reductionists; they argue that there mental properties exist, but these are in fact physical. Talk of the mental can be ONTOLOGICALLY REDUCED to talk of the physical.	Eliminativists are not reductionists; they are not merely claiming that when we talk about minds we really mean brains – instead, they claim that mental states *do not exist*.

Denial of qualia

The INTENTIONALIST approach to consciousness argues that 'conscious states' are just intentional states (states which possess INTENTIONALITY).

Eliminativists suggest that the difficulty with such an approach is that qualia don't seem to possess intentionality – the pain of a headache doesn't represent anything; it just hurts. So qualia seem to be an aspect of consciousness over and above mere intentional content. The headache may cause me to have the thought "I am in pain" (an intentional thought) but the pain itself is a non-intentional aspect of the experience. According to intentionalism, mental states therefore can't be reduced to intentional states.

Dennett – an eliminativist – responds to the intentionalist approach by denying that qualia exist at all; he suggests that qualia are just an illusion. Dennett doesn't deny that we really do have conscious experiences – feeling pain, tasting apple pie, smelling perfume, hearing music – but he denies that any of these experiences feature INTRINSIC or subjective properties. Dennett maintains that folk psychology is just a theory and qualia are theoretical; we can't be sure that they exist.

Inverted qualia Dennett puts forward a thought experiment (see right panel) where we appear to have INVERTED QUALIA. He suggests that if such an experience were to happen to you, the only way to find out why you are having these experiences would be to ask the surgeons, or to study your neural patterns. Either way, it shows that qualia are not FIRST-PERSONAL and subjective, because you'd have to rely on objective information to tell you what was going on. This shows that qualia do not have an intrinsic nature, as we can't be sure of them.	Imagine you have brain surgery, and when you wake up, you are shocked to discover that grass now looks red, ladybirds look green, and the sky looks orange. You can't tell whether the brain surgeons have tampered with your memory of colours, or whether they have tampered with how your brain processes colours right now. In other words, you aren't sure whether things look the same as always and you are misremembering how they used to look, or whether your memory is accurate but you are now having new experiences of the colours of things.

Note that Dennett isn't arguing that we don't have any qualia – he is merely suggesting that qualia aren't first-personal and subjective. If we were in the thought experiment, we would of course be having qualia, (of the grass appearing red etc.) but we wouldn't know through INTROSPECTION whether our qualia were genuine or had been altered.

Folk psychology

FOLK PSYCHOLOGY is simply what average, everyday people believe about psychology (i.e. our ways of thinking). We have intuitions and ideas about psychology which, because we are not experts, may not be completely correct. Paul Churchland and Patricia Churchland argue that we should abandon folk psychology because it is false (or at least, radically mistaken), and we should replace it with a neuroscientific theory and vocabulary.

Why eliminate talk of the mind?

Eliminative materialists argue that we should eliminate talk about mental states from our language, since mental states don't exist. It might seem odd to eliminate talk of the mind, but throughout history we have abandoned talk of ideas which have been found to be false.

For example, scientists used to talk about phlogiston (a chemical thought to be released when something burns), and doctors used to talk about balancing the 'four humours' (blood, phlegm, black bile and yellow bile). Now we have realised that these ideas were misinformed, and the terminologies describing the non-existent things have been eliminated from our language.

Similarly, eliminativists argue that qualia and other mental states do not exist, and should thus be eliminated from our language along with talk of phlogiston and the four humours.

We should abandon folk psychology

Paul and Patricia Churchland note that folk psychology is an empirical theory which we use to predict and explain others' behaviour, but it is very inaccurate. We should eliminate terms associated with inaccurate folk psychology, and embrace more accurate terms from neuroscience. Their argument can be summarised as:

1. Folk psychology is false (or at least, radically misleading)
2. Neuroscience is accurate (or at least, more accurate than folk psychology)
3. We should abandon false or misleading theories in favour of ones which are more accurate
4. Therefore, we should abandon folk psychology in favour of neuroscience
5. When accepting a theory, one should adopt its terminology

C. Therefore, we should adopt neuroscientific terminology, and eliminate folk psychological terminology of mental states

Although the Churchlands are right that neuroscience is more accurate than folk psychology (premises 1 and 2), premises 3-5 are excessive. There are many theories (e.g. quantum mechanics, sociolinguistics, or palaeontology) which are more precise than our general knowledge of these fields. However, it is unrealistic to expect everyone to fully understand the terminology used in these fields, and to abandon their everyday language about objects, language, or evolution.

The same is true in the case of neuroscience as compared to our folk psychological talk about minds: our words are imprecise and imperfect, but the terminology works well enough in our everyday lives.

Strengths

- It is true to claim that neuroscience is more accurate and precise in its language than folk psychology is, when referring to mental events.
- The Churchlands may be correct that *some* people do not have qualia, as shown in Chalmers' PHILOSOPHICAL ZOMBIE ARGUMENT (p114).

Strength

- Some phrases from biology have entered our everyday language, such as 'having an adrenaline rush'.

Criticisms

- Arguments in favour of eliminativism seem to rely on mental states: Dennett *believes* that eliminativism is correct; Churchland *hopes* that people will abandon talk of the mental – so eliminativism seems self-defeating!
- Even though neuroscience is more precise and well-informed than folk psychology, we cannot expect everyone to become neuroscientific experts and to abandon their everyday language.
- Language is organic and ever-evolving; in time, people may abandon words like 'hope', 'remember' and 'feel' in favour of talk about particular chemicals being released in the brain, but this will happen slowly over time; we cannot expect people to do it straight away.
- Folk psychology has good predictive and explanatory power; it is often right about things, and so provides us with the BEST HYPOTHESIS.

Criticisms

- I am certain that I have mental states and qualia, and this takes priority over other considerations such as the weaknesses of folk psychology; no one can convince me that my qualia do not exist.
- The terminology and understanding of folk psychology serves people very well; most people can have successful lives without requiring knowledge of neuroscience.
- Dennett's inverted qualia thought experiment doesn't show that qualia don't exist – only that, in exceptional circumstances, they may be mistaken about the nature of reality.

Response: The example shows that qualia aren't always subjective or first personal.

- The eliminativists may be right that there is nothing which corresponds to the feeling of a quale – but that may be because qualia are INEFFABLE, FIRST-PERSONAL, and only accessible through INTROSPECTION, so there is no way to explain them to anyone else; we needn't conclude that qualia don't exist.

Functionalism

Overview

Key philosophers: Searle, Block

Unlike SUBSTANCE DUALISM or IDENTITY THEORY, functionalism identifies a mind in terms of how it functions, rather than what it is made of. This means that functionalism can be compatible with substance dualism and MATERIALISM. Functionalism is an approach which maintains that mental states can be characterised in terms of their functions.

We often categorise things by their function rather than what they are made of – foods, transport, bottle openers, and so on. For example, a metal fork, a plastic spoon, and wooden chopsticks are all cutlery, because their function is to help people eat.

Multiple realisability

Functionalists maintain that if something *functions* like a mind, then it is a mind. So a mind can be a human brain – but it could also be a group of silicon chips in a robot, or some green slime in the chest of an alien – it could even be a non-physical mental substance. The fact that mental states are MULTIPLY REALISABLE is the cornerstone of functionalism, not a criticism of it.

The façade of a mind

Functionalism shares some features with behaviourism, because it is based on how beings act or function – but it is also vulnerable to some of the criticisms of behaviourism. In particular, the problem that something can *appear* to have a mind when in fact it does not.

The Turing test

The TURING TEST, designed by computer scientist Alan Turing, is a way of determining whether a computer has a mind. Two people and a computer have a text-based conversation where they send messages to each other. If the people cannot tell which is the computer and which is the other person, then the computer has passed the test and is said to have a mind.

The Chinese Room

The CHINESE ROOM is a criticism of the Turing test (and functionalism in general) by Searle. A man who doesn't understand Chinese is in a room with a book. The book says things like "when you are passed these symbols 玩狟鼅 then you should respond with these symbols 不觉玫." But the book doesn't tell the man what the symbols mean in English. Someone passes a message in Chinese symbols to the man, and the man follows the book's instructions and passes a message out.

To the people on the outside of the room, it *appears* that the man understands Chinese, but he does not.

After a long time in the Chinese room, when particular symbols are passed in to the man, he would automatically know which symbols to respond with. In this way, he could get to a point where he no longer requires the book, and he can function (in writing) as someone who understands Chinese perfectly – but still he does not understand it.

A problem for functionalism is that in characterising a mind in terms of its functions, we can have something which appears to have a mind (or a particular mental state) when it doesn't. The man functions as someone who understands Chinese, and a machine can appear to function as if it has a mind, when really it does not.

The Chinese mind

Block puts forward the CHINESE MIND argument (also known as the 'Chinese nation'; or 'China head' argument) as a criticism of functionalism. It can be summarised as:

Imagine that an enormous number of people, such as the population of China (1.4bn people) interact with each other exactly like neurones in the brain; they send basic messages to each other. Imagine that this network is connected to a robotic body (or a 'China-head'), so that when the robot is hit, the people of China send signals to one another as would happen in a human brain. Signals are then sent back to the robot, and this causes the robot to say "Ouch!"

The Chinese mind lacks any qualia, even though it supposedly functions exactly the same as the human brain does (and the robot body supposedly functions the same as a human body does). The body is hit, signals are sent between 'neurones' and then 'ouch!' is said – but the robot does not *feel* pain, and the people of China as a whole do not have a single consciousness.

This is intended to demonstrate that *functioning* as a mind is not the same as *being* a mind.

***A note on Chinese minds and rooms**: Despite both arguments referring to 'Chinese' something, the arguments are unrelated to one another (except that they both criticise functionalism). The room was (probably) chosen to be Chinese because the traditional Chinese language is one of the most difficult in the world. The mind was chosen to be Chinese because China is the most populous country on Earth. The two arguments do not criticise one another.*

Strengths

- Functionalism can fit with dualism, because if a non-physical substance functions like it has a mind, then it is a mind.
- Functionalism can fit with physicalism, because if a physical substance such as a brain functions like it has a mind, then it is a mind.
- It accounts for multiple realisability, which was a problem for IDENTITY THEORY and BEHAVIOURISM.
- It accepts the view that minds need not be (human) brains but could instead be an artificial intelligence or alien; this fits with scientific thinking about the development of artificial intelligence.
- Functionalism can account for people with conditions such as 'locked in syndrome' where their brain functions normally, but they are unable to move; according to functionalism, these people still have minds.

Criticisms

- It is possible for a ZOMBIE to exist, which functions as if it has a mind, when in fact it does not. There would be no way to tell the difference between a zombie and a minded person, so mindedness cannot be solely about function.

Criticisms

- It is possible for there to be another person who is exactly the same as me functionally (a 'FUNCTIONAL DUPLICATE') but with different qualia – for example, what he calls red, I would call green, and what he calls savoury, I would call sweet. We have 'INVERTED QUALIA' but we would never know. This possibility means that there is more to a mental state than its mere function.

Response: This is unimportant; both people would be functioning as though they experience qualia and have minds, and so the theory of functionalism is still plausible.

- Functionalism struggles to explain qualia because there is more to a quale than merely its function; the experience of consciousness is INEFFABLE and not solely about function. When Mary escapes her black and white room (see p116) she has new qualia that cannot be understood in terms of function.
- If we came across an alien (or Earth animal) with a physiology completely different to ours, it would be difficult (if not impossible) to determine whether it has something which functions as a mind; we may have to simply observe its behaviour, which is problematic (see p127).

Criticisms

- Block's Chinese mind argument shows that something can mimic the functions of the brain and body (a 'functional duplicate') but lack any qualia.

Response: It is not clear that the population of China sending messages to one another really *does* mimic the functions of a brain; the example is problematic because it uses a group of people, each of whom has a mind of his own. If the argument were about a series of computer chips, we would perhaps say that it *does* have a mind.

- Searle's Chinese room demonstrates that something can function as if it understands language when in fact it does not. Similarly, something can function as if it has a mind when in fact it does not.

Response: Some philosophers suggest that the man in the Chinese room (together with the book) *does* understand Chinese, as he can converse in it and is 'fluent'. Similarly, we have 'rules' in our minds that when someone says X, an appropriate reply is Y, and there's no difference, except that the man's 'rules' are written in a book instead of in his mind.

Specification Content

The following information is from the AQA A Level Philosophy specification, which can be found at:
http://www.aqa.org.uk/subjects/philosophy/as-and-a-level/philosophy-7172

Metaphysics of God

1a The concept and nature of 'God'

God's attributes:

- God as omniscient, omnipotent, supremely good (omnibenevolent), and the meaning(s) of these divine attributes
- Competing views on such a being's relationship to time, including God being timeless (eternal) and God being within time (everlasting)
- Arguments for the incoherence of the concept of God including:
  - the paradox of the stone
  - the Euthyphro dilemma
  - the compatibility, or otherwise, of the existence of an omniscient God and free human beings

1b Arguments relating to the existence of God

For the arguments below, students should pay particular attention to nuances in the logical form of the arguments (deductive, inductive etc), the strengths of the conclusions (God does exist, God must exist etc) and the nature of God assumed or defended by the argument

Ontological arguments

- St Anselm's ontological argument
- Descartes' ontological argument
- Norman Malcolm's ontological argument

Issues that may arise for the arguments above, including:

- Gaunilo's 'perfect island' objection
- Empiricist objections to *a priori* arguments for existence
- Kant's objection based on existence not being a predicate

Teleological/design arguments

- The design argument from analogy (as presented by Hume)

- William Paley's design argument: argument from spatial order/purpose
- Richard Swinburne's design argument: argument from temporal order/regularity

Issues that may arise for the arguments above, including:

- Hume's objections to the design argument from analogy
- The problem of spatial disorder (as posed by Hume and Paley)
- The design argument fails as it is an argument from a unique case (Hume)
- Whether God is the best or only explanation

Cosmological arguments

- The Kalam argument (an argument from temporal causation)
- Aquinas' first way (argument from motion), second way (argument from atemporal causation) and third way (an argument from contingency)
- Descartes' argument based on his continuing existence (an argument from causation)
- Leibniz's argument from the principle of sufficient reason (an argument from contingency)

Issues that may arise for the arguments above, including:

- The possibility of an infinite series
- Hume's objection to the 'causal principle'
- The argument commits the fallacy of composition (Russell)
- The impossibility of a necessary being (Hume and Russell)

The Problem of Evil

Whether God's attributes can be reconciled with the existence of evil

- The nature of moral evil and natural evil
- The logical and evidential forms of the problem of evil

Responses to these issues, and issues arising from these responses, including:

- The Free Will Defence (including Alvin Plantinga)
- Soul-making (including John Hick)

1c Religious language

- The distinction between cognitivism and non-cognitivism about religious language

- The empiricist/logical positivist challenges to the status of metaphysical (here, religious) language: the verification principle and verification/falsification (Ayer)
- Hick's response to Ayer (eschatological verification) and issues arising from that response

Further responses: the 'University Debate'

- Anthony Flew on falsification (Wisdom's 'Gardener')
- Basil Mitchell's response to Flew (the Partisan)
- Hare's response to Flew (bliks and the lunatic)

and issues arising from those responses

Metaphysics of Mind

2a What do we mean by 'mind'?

Features of mental states:

- All or at least some mental states have phenomenal properties
- Some, but not all, philosophers use the term 'qualia' to refer to these properties, where 'qualia' are defined as 'intrinsic and non-intentional phenomenal properties that are introspectively accessible'
- All or at least some mental states have intentional properties (i.e. intentionality)

2b Dualist theories

Substance dualism

- Minds exist and are not identical to bodies or to parts of bodies
- The indivisibility argument for substance dualism (Descartes)

Responses, including:

- The mental is divisible in some sense
- Not everything thought of as physical is divisible

The conceivability argument for substance dualism (expressed without reference to God) (Descartes)

Responses including:

- Mind without body is not conceivable
- What is conceivable may not be metaphysically possible
- What is metaphysically possible tells us nothing about the actual world

Property dualism

- There are at least some mental properties that are neither reducible to nor supervenient upon physical properties
- The 'philosophical zombies' argument for property dualism (David Chalmers)

Responses including:

- A 'philosophical zombie'/a 'zombie' world is not conceivable
- What is conceivable may not be metaphysically possible
- What is metaphysically possible tells us nothing about the actual world

The 'knowledge/Mary' argument for property dualism (Frank Jackson)

Responses including:

- Mary does not gain new propositional knowledge but does gain ability knowledge (the 'ability knowledge' response)
- Mary does not gain new propositional knowledge but does gain acquaintance knowledge (the 'acquaintance knowledge' response)
- Mary gains new propositional knowledge, but this is knowledge of physical facts that she already knew in a different way (the 'New Knowledge / Old Fact' response)

Issues

Issues facing dualism, including:

- The problem of other minds

Responses, including:

- The argument from analogy
- The existence of other minds is the best hypothesis

Dualism makes a "category mistake" (Gilbert Ryle)

Issues facing interactionist dualism, including:

- The conceptual interaction problem (as articulated by Elisabeth, Princess of Bohemia)
- The empirical interaction problem

Issues facing epiphenomenalist dualism, including:

- The challenge posed by introspective self-knowledge
- The challenge posed by the phenomenology of our mental life (i.e. as involving causal connections, both psychological and psycho-physical)
- The challenge posed by natural selection/evolution

2c Physicalist theories

Physicalism

Everything is physical or supervenes upon the physical (this includes properties, events, objects and any substance(s) that exist)

Philosophical behaviourism:

- 'Hard' behaviourism: all propositions about mental states can be reduced without loss of meaning to propositions that exclusively use the language of physics to talk about bodily states/movements (including Carl Hempel)
- 'Soft' behaviourism: propositions about mental states are propositions about behavioural dispositions (i.e. propositions that use ordinary language) (including Gilbert Ryle)

Issues including:

- Dualist arguments applied to philosophical behaviourism
- The distinctness of mental states from behaviour (including Hilary Putnam's 'super-Spartans' and perfect actors)
- Issues defining mental states satisfactorily due to (a) circularity and (b) the multiple realisability of mental states in behaviour
- The asymmetry between self-knowledge and knowledge of other people

Mind-brain type identity theory

- All mental states are identical to brain states ('ontological' reduction) although 'mental state' and 'brain state' are not synonymous (so not an 'analytic' reduction)

Issues including:

- Dualist arguments applied to mind-brain type identity theory
- Issues with providing the type identities (the multiple realisability of mental states)

Eliminative materialism

- Some or all common-sense ("folk-psychological") mental states/properties do not exist and our common-sense understanding is radically mistaken (as defended by Patricia Churchland and Paul Churchland)

Issues including:

- Our certainty about the existence of our mental states takes priority over other considerations

- Folk-psychology has good predictive and explanatory power (and so is the best hypothesis)
- The articulation of eliminative materialism as a theory is self-refuting

2d Functionalism

- All mental states can be characterised in terms of functional roles which can be multiply realised

Issues, including:

- The possibility of a functional duplicate with different qualia (inverted qualia)
- The possibility of a functional duplicate with no mentality/qualia (Ned Block's China thought experiment)
- The 'knowledge'/Mary argument can be applied to functional facts (no amount of facts about function suffices to explain qualia)

Possible Exam Questions

Listed below are some possible exam questions. The list is not exhaustive, as other questions can appear on an exam paper. However, it should give you a useful idea of the sorts of questions you might be asked in the Paper 2 exam.

Metaphysics of God

3 mark questions

1. Briefly explain what it means to say that God is omniscient. *(3 marks)*
2. Briefly explain the principle of sufficient reason. *(3 marks)*
3. Briefly explain what is meant by 'death by a thousand qualifications'. *(3 marks)*
4. Briefly explain the Euthyphro dilemma. *(3 marks)*
5. Briefly explain what Kant means when he argues that existence is not a predicate. *(3 marks)*
6. Briefly explain what is meant by 'natural evil'. *(3 marks)*
7. Briefly explain the verification principle. *(3 marks)*
8. Briefly explain what is meant by the term 'unmoved mover'. *(3 marks)*
9. Briefly explain the paradox of the stone. *(3 marks)*
10. Briefly explain the difference between everlasting and eternal, as competing attributes of God. *(3 marks)*

5 mark questions

1. Outline Malcolm's ontological argument for the existence of God. *(5 marks)*
2. Explain the Kalam argument. *(5 marks)*
3. Explain Leibniz's cosmological argument. *(5 marks)*
4. Explain the differences between the logical and evidential problems of evil. *(5 marks)*
5. Explain Aquinas' third way (an argument from contingency). *(5 marks)*
6. Explain what Hare means by 'bliks'. *(5 marks)*
7. Outline why logical positivists suggest that religious language is not meaningful. *(5 marks)*
8. Outline Flew's parable of the invisible gardener. *(5 marks)*

9. Explain the difference between moral and natural evil. *(5 marks)*
10. Explain Hick's soul-making theodicy. *(5 marks)*

12 mark questions

1. Outline two of Hume's objections to the design argument from analogy. *(12 marks)*
2. Compare and contrast verification and falsification as approaches to religious language. *(12 marks)*
3. Outline and explain the paradox of the stone, and one possible solution to it. *(12 marks)*
4. Compare and contrast Hick's soul-making theodicy and Plantinga's free will defence. *(12 marks)*
5. Outline and explain two criticisms of the claim that God is omniscient. *(12 marks)*
6. Outline and explain two criticisms of the Kalam argument. *(12 marks)*
7. Compare and contrast cosmological arguments and ontological arguments. *(12 marks)*
8. Outline and explain Gaunilo's response to Anselm's ontological argument. *(12 marks)*
9. Compare and contrast the teleological argument from spatial order/purpose and the teleological argument from temporal order/regularity. *(12 marks)*
10. Outline and explain what is meant by the claim that religious statements are eschatologically verifiable. *(12 marks)*

25 mark questions

1. Does the problem of evil successfully demonstrate that an omnibenevolent God does not exist? *(25 marks)*
2. How convincing are ontological arguments for the existence of God? *(25 marks)*
3. Are God's attributes coherent? *(25 marks)*
4. Are teleological arguments successful in demonstrating that God designed the universe? *(25 marks)*
5. Critically assess the claim that Aquinas demonstrates that God exists. *(25 marks)*
6. If God is omniscient, are human beings free? *(25 marks)*
7. Critically assess the claim that cosmological arguments are convincing. *(25 marks)*

8. Do the logical positivists demonstrate that religious language is meaningless? *(25 marks)*
9. Can there really be an omnipotent God? *(25 marks)*
10. Critically assess the claim that the Euthyphro dilemma cannot be solved. *(25 marks)*

Metaphysics of Mind

3 mark questions

1. Briefly explain the eliminative materialist claim that all talk of mental states can and should be eliminated. *(3 marks)*
2. Briefly explain property dualism. *(3 marks)*
3. Briefly explain functionalism. *(3 marks)*
4. Briefly explain the masked man fallacy. *(3 marks)*
5. Briefly explain the argument from analogy relating to other minds. *(3 marks)*
6. Briefly explain what philosophers mean when they claim that mental events have 'intentional properties'. *(3 marks)*
7. Briefly explain epiphenomenalist dualism. *(3 marks)*
8. Briefly explain the 'inverted qualia' criticism of functionalism. *(3 marks)*
9. Briefly explain the difference between soft behaviourism and hard behaviourism. *(3 marks)*
10. Briefly explain the conceivability argument for substance dualism. *(3 marks)*

5 mark questions

1. Outline one physicalist criticism of substance dualism. *(5 marks)*
2. Explain how one might criticise Descartes' conceivability argument by arguing that the conceivable may not be possible. *(5 marks)*
3. Explain why multiple realisability is a problem for hard behaviourism. *(5 marks)*
4. Outline the 'zombie' argument for property dualism. *(5 marks)*
5. Explain why the causal redundancy of the mental is a problem for epiphenomenalist dualism. *(5 marks)*
6. Explain Ryle's argument that dualism rests on a 'category mistake'. *(5 marks)*

7. Explain the difference between mind-brain type identity theory and mind-brain token identity theory. *(5 marks)*
8. Explain the inverted qualia criticism of functionalism. *(5 marks)*
9. Outline Block's 'Chinese mind' argument. *(5 marks)*
10. Explain why the articulation of eliminative materialism may be self-refuting. *(5 marks)*

12 mark questions

1. Outline and explain two criticisms of identity theory. *(12 marks)*
2. Compare and contrast ontological reduction and analytic reduction. *(12 marks)*
3. Outline and explain two criticisms of functionalism. *(12 marks)*
4. Outline the knowledge / Mary argument for property dualism, and explain why it might be said that Mary gains no new knowledge when she is released. *(12 marks)*
5. Compare and contrast substance dualism and property dualism. *(12 marks)*
6. Outline and explain two criticisms of the indivisibility argument. *(12 marks)*
7. Outline and explain two criticisms of soft behaviourism. *(12 marks)*
8. Compare and contrast interactionist dualism and epiphenomenalist dualism. *(12 marks)*
9. Outline and explain one strength and one criticism of the claim that the existence of other minds is the 'best hypothesis'. *(12 marks)*
10. Outline the philosophical zombie argument for property dualism, and explain one criticism of it. *(12 marks)*

25 mark questions

1. Should we eliminate all talk of the mind? *(25 marks)*
2. Critically assess the claim that the interaction problem faced by substance dualism cannot be solved. *(25 marks)*
3. Critically assess the claim that the mind supervenes on the brain but cannot be reduced to it. *(25 marks)*
4. Do qualia exist? *(25 marks)*
5. Critically assess the claim that other humans have minds. *(25 marks)*
6. Should the mind be defined in terms of its functions? *(25 marks)*
7. Critically assess the claim that the mind is the human brain. *(25 marks)*

8. Critically assess the extent to which Descartes' arguments demonstrate that the mind can exist independently of the brain. *(25 marks)*
9. Assess the extent to which the a zombie world is possible. *(25 marks)*
10. Critically assess the behaviourist account of the mind. *(25 marks)*

List of Philosophers

Below is a chronological list of the philosophers whose arguments are contained within this book.

Socrates (469-399 BCE)

Plato (427-347 BCE)

Aristotle (384-322 BCE)

Epicurus (341-270 BCE)

Irenaeus (130-202 AD)

Augustine, St. (354-430 AD)

Gaunilo (circa 1030 AD)

Anselm, St. (1033-1109)

Al-Ghazali (1058-1111)

Averroes (1126-1198)

Aquinas, St. Thomas (1225-1274)

Descartes, René (1596-1650)

Arnauld, Antoine (1612-1694)

Princess of Bohemia, Elisabeth (1618-80)

Leibniz, Gottfried Wilhelm (1646-1716)

Hume, David (1711-1776)

Kant, Immanuel (1724-1804)

Paley, William (1743-1805)

Schopenhauer, Arthur (1788-1860)

Kierkegaard, Søren (1813-1855)

Russell, Bertrand (1872-1970)

Wittgenstein, Ludwig (1889-1951)

Ryle, Gilbert (1900-1976)

Hempel, Carl (1905-1997)

Sartre, Jean-Paul (1905-1980)

Ayer, A. J. (1910-1989)

Malcolm, Norman (1911-1990)

Mackie, J. L. (1917-1981)

Mitchell, Basil (1917-2011)

Hare, R. M. (1919-2002)

Smart, J. J. C. (1920-2012)

Hick, John (1922-2012)

Flew, Antony (1923-2010)

Putnam, Hilary (1926-2016)

Mavrodes, George (1926-)

Kretzmann, Norman (1928-1998)

Kenny, Anthony (1931-)

Searle, John (1932-)

Plantinga, Alvin (1932-)

Swinburne, Richard (1934-)

Savage, C. W. (circa 1940-)

Lewis, David (1941-2001)

Dennett, Daniel (1942-)

Churchland, Paul (1942-)

Block, Ned (1942-)

Jackson, Frank (1943-)

Churchland, Patricia (1943-)

Chalmers, David (1966-)

Set Texts and Further Reading

Metaphysics of God

Anselm, St. *Proslogium*, [Chapters II–IV and Gaunilo, from the appendix to Anselm's *Proslogium*]

Aquinas, T. *Summa Theologica* [Part 1, Question 25, Article 3 and Question 2, Article 3]

Ayer, A.J. (1946) *Language, Truth and Logic* [Chapters 1 and 6]

Ayer, A.J. (1973) *The Central Questions of Philosophy*, pp22–29

Descartes, R. (1641) *Meditations on First Philosophy* [Meditations 3 and 5]

Flew, A., Hare, R.M. and Mitchell, B. (1955) 'Theology and Falsification' in *New Essays in Philosophical Theology*, edited by Flew, A. and MacIntyre, A.

Hick, J. (1966) *Evil and the God of Love* [Chapters 13–17 (esp chapter 13)]

Hume, D. (1779) *Dialogues Concerning Natural Religion* [Parts II, V, VIII and IX]

Hume, D. (1748) *Enquiry Concerning Human Understanding* [Part XI]

Leibniz, G.W. (1714) *Monadology* [Sections 32–39]

Malcolm, N. (1960) 'Anselm's ontological arguments', *The Philosophical Review*, 69, 41 62

Midgley, M. (1984) *Wickedness* [Chapters 1 and 5]

Paley, W. (1802) *Natural Theology* [Chapters 1, 2 and 5]

Plantinga, A. (1975) *God, Freedom and Evil: Essays in Philosophy* [pp29–34 and 59–64]

Plato, *Euthyphro*

Stump, E. and Kretzmann, N. (1981) 'Eternity', *Journal of Philosophy* 78 (8): 429–458

Swinburne, R.G. (1968) 'The Argument from Design', *Philosophy*, 43 (165): 199–212

Metaphysics of Mind

Avramides, A. (2001) *Other Minds* [Chapter 2]

Block, N. (1980) 'Troubles with functionalism', in *Readings in Philosophy of Psychology*, Vol 1 [Section 1–2]

Chalmers, D. (1996) *The Conscious Mind: In Search of a Fundamental Theory* [Chapter 1]

Chalmers, D. (2003) 'Consciousness and its place in nature' in *The Blackwell Guide to the Philosophy of Mind* [Sections 2 and 3]

Churchland, P.S. (2002) *Brain-wise* [Introduction (Sections 1, 3, 4) and Chapter 4, (Section 2)]

Churchland, P. (1981) 'Eliminative Materialism and Propositional Attitudes', *Journal of Philosophy* 78, 67–90 [Section 2]

Descartes, R. (1641) *Meditations on First Philosophy* [Meditation 6]

Hempel, C. (1949) 'The Logical Analysis of Psychology'. in Jeffrey, R. (Ed) *Hempel: Selected Philosophical Essays*

Jackson, F. (1982) 'Epiphenomenal Qualia', *Philosophical quarterly*, 32, 127–136

Putnam, H. (1975) 'The Nature of Mental States' in *Mind, Language and Reality: Philosophical Papers, Volume 2*

Ryle, G. (1949) *The Concept of Mind* [Chapters 1, 2, 5 and 6]

Shapiro, L. (Ed) (2007) *The correspondence between Princess Elisabeth of Bohemia and René Descartes*, edited and translated [Letters from May 1643]

Smart, J.J.C. (1959) 'Sensations and brain processes', *The Philosophical Review*, 68 (2), 141–156

Glossary

A posteriori: something that can only be known through experience, e.g. that grass is green (contrast with A PRIORI)

A priori: something that can be known through REASON (INTUITION or DEDUCTION), e.g. that 2 + 3 = 5 or that "all bachelors are unmarried" (contrast with A POSTERIORI)

Abductive argument: an ARGUMENT which uses ABDUCTIVE REASONING. If the premises are true, the conclusion is supposedly the best explanation of them (contrast with DEDUCTIVE or INDUCTIVE ARGUMENTS)

Abductive reasoning: an INFERENCE TO THE BEST EXPLANATION – choosing the theory which best explains the data, even though it is not guaranteed to be true (contrast with INDUCTIVE or DEDUCTIVE REASONING)

Ability knowledge: knowing how to do something, e.g. knowing how to ride a bike (contrast with ACQUAINTANCE or PROPOSITIONAL KNOWLEDGE)

Acquaintance knowledge: knowing a person or thing, e.g. "I know Dave" means you recognise him and/or know things about him (contrast with ABILITY or PROPOSITIONAL KNOWLEDGE)

Actually impossible: something which is not possible in the real world as we know it, e.g. for a man to jump 100 metres (contrast with ACTUALLY POSSIBLE or LOGICALLY IMPOSSIBLE)

Actually possible: something which is possible in the real world, e.g. for a man to run a marathon in 4 hours (contrast with LOGICALLY POSSIBLE or ACTUALLY IMPOSSIBLE)

Ad hominem: a weak way of arguing which involves criticising the speaker rather than criticising their argument

Affirming the consequent: a logical FALLACY which takes the form: "If P then Q. Q. Therefore P." (contrast with MODUS PONENS) (see DENYING THE ANTECEDENT)

All possible worlds: every single different variation of how the universe could have turned out. All CONTINGENT truths can be different in another possible world, but NECESSARY truths must remain the same in all possible worlds

Analytic reduction: when one set of terms can be used interchangeably with another simpler set of terms (contrast with ONTOLOGICAL REDUCTION)

Analytical behaviourism: see SOFT BEHAVIOURISM

Analytically false: a proposition whose falsity can be known A PRIORI, simply by understanding the meanings of the words, e.g. "All spinsters are married" (contrast with ANALYTICALLY TRUE or SYNTHETICALLY FALSE)

Analytically true: a proposition whose truth can be known A PRIORI, simply by understanding the meanings of the words, e.g. "All spinsters are unmarried" (contrast with ANALYTICALLY FALSE or SYNTHETICALLY TRUE)

Anomalous monism: PHYSICALIST theory that mental states are identical to brain states, but that there cannot be any laws of nature governing them, because people differ from one another (also see MIND-BRAIN-TOKEN IDENTITY THEORY)

Antecedent: the "if" part of a CONDITIONAL (if-then) statement, e.g. in the statement "If it's Monday, then I have a Philosophy lesson", the antecedent is "If it's Monday" (contrast with CONSEQUENT)

Anthropic principle: given that we exist, it is unremarkable that the universe (or Earth) is capable of supporting life – just as the odds against any one person existing are astronomical, yet here we all are

Argument from analogy: an argument which draws an analogy with some other topic, person or area of study in order to make a point about the area in question. Mill draws an analogy about others' minds based on his own; Paley draws an analogy between a watch designer and a universe designer

Argument from causation: Aquinas' second proof of God – a COSMOLOGICAL ARGUMENT – suggesting that everything has a cause, and the first cause of everything is God

Argument from conceivability: Descartes' argument that it's conceivable (LOGICALLY POSSIBLE) for the mind and body to be distinct from one another

Argument from contingency: Leibniz's and Aquinas' COSMOLOGICAL ARGUMENTS that the universe is CONTINGENT, and cannot be explained by something else contingent, so there must be a NECESSARY BEING which created everything

Argument from design: theory that God exists because only he could have designed the universe to work so perfectly

Argument from design qua purpose: Paley's argument that physical wonders such as the human eye work so well they must have been designed by an intelligent being with a purpose in mind; this INTELLIGENT DESIGNER is God

Argument from design qua regularity: Swinburne's argument that cause and effect are temporal wonders, and the laws of motion etc. must have been designed by an intelligent being; this INTELLIGENT DESIGNER is God

Argument from indivisibility: Descartes' argument that the brain and body can be divided into smaller pieces, whereas the mind cannot. This supports the claim that the mind is not the brain

Argument from introspection: criticism of EPIPHENOMENALIST DUALISM, that I know my mental states via self-reflection, but this would not be possible if my mental states didn't cause anything (my thoughts cause other thoughts when I reflect)

Argument from motion: Aquinas' first proof of God, arguing that everything that moves must have a mover, and the first mover of everything is God

Argument: provides reasons or evidence in support of a CONCLUSION; a course of reasoning aimed at demonstrating a truth or falsehood; the methodical process of logical reasoning

Aseity: a possible attribute of God: that he does not depend on anything else for his existence

Assertion: stating something as if it is a fact (sometimes without any evidence)

Atemporal: existing outside of time (see ETERNAL) (contrast with TEMPORAL)

Atheism: belief that there is no God

Attacking a straw man: distorting or misrepresenting your opponent's argument, and then criticising that distorted argument e.g. "Paley argues that God designed the universe and watches, but God didn't design watches, so this is an unconvincing argument..."

Begging the question: when the PREMISE(S) in an argument rely on believing the CONCLUSION; when an argument makes an assumption which an opponent would object to, e.g. "I have witnessed a miracle, therefore miracles are real"

Behaviourism: theory suggesting that mindedness simply *is* behaviour; we can replace talk about the mind with talk about behaviour (see HARD BEHAVIOURISM and SOFT BEHAVIOURISM)

Belief: an opinion or view that something is true

Benevolence: kindness; goodness; doing good things for others; sometimes used to mean OMNIBENEVOLENCE

Big Bang: scientific theory that the universe began with an explosion of matter which continues expanding today; prior to the Big Bang, there was no space or time

Big Crunch: scientific theory that once the universe has finished expanding, it will begin contracting, and it will all squash together again and collapse into a black hole (see CYCLIC MODEL)

Blik: word coined by Hare to mean a belief or conviction which is not FALSIFIABLE because the speaker believes it so deeply – but it is still meaningful

Burden of proof: the obligation to prove a specific claim (rather than relying on others to disprove it). E.g. if I claimed that my dog was Elvis reincarnated, the burden of proof would lie with me – I would be expected to prove he *is* Elvis; it's not the job of other people to prove he is *not* Elvis

Cartesian: developed by or referring to Descartes

Category mistake: a fallacy which involves placing something into the wrong category (e.g. the tourist sees all the Colleges and Halls in Oxford, yet he still asks "but where is the university?")

Causal adequacy principle: Descartes' claim that the cause of something must be at least as real and perfect as the effect

Causal closure (of the physical universe): the physical universe can only be affected by things which are within the physical universe; non-physical entities cannot cause anything physical

Causally redundant: not causing anything

Causally inert: unable to cause anything

Certainty: a very strongly held belief (see INFALLIBLE beliefs)

Chinese head: Block's example of the population of China sending signals between one another as neurones in the brain do, and being connected to a robot. Together they lack any qualia, but function as a brain

Chinese room: criticism of the TURING TEST: a man is in a room with a book showing Chinese characters; it says if someone passes you these symbols: 音牱㞍 then pass them these symbols: 坙黖 The man appears to understand Chinese, when in fact he doesn't really understand it

Circularity / circular argument: an unsatisfactory type of ARGUMENT where the CONCLUSION merely restates a PREMISE or refers back to the premise, e.g. "The Bible is the word of God. We know this because it says so in the Bible."

Cognitivism: theory that when we make religious statements such as "God lives in all of us" we are articulating our beliefs, but we are not saying anything FACTUALLY MEANINGFUL (contrast with NON-COGNITIVISM) (also see LOGICAL POSITIVISM and the VERIFICATION PRINCIPLE)

Communicable attributes of God: attributes which human beings can also have, e.g. goodness (contrast with INCOMMUNICABLE ATTRIBUTES)

Conceivability argument: see ARGUMENT FROM CONCEIVABILITY

Conclusion: the end point of a logical ARGUMENT or SYLLOGISM; usually appears as the last line, and often indicated by the word "therefore"

Conditional: an if-then statement e.g. "If you love your wife, then don't hit her"

Consciousness: our subjective awareness of the world and our mental states

Consequent: the "then" part of a CONDITIONAL (if-then) statement, e.g. in the statement "If it's Monday, then I have a Philosophy lesson", the consequent is "then I have a philosophy lesson" (contrast with ANTECEDENT)

Contingent being: a being which exists, but might not have done; one whose existence depends on something else in the world (e.g. my existence depended on my parents meeting each other) (contrast with a NECESSARY BEING)

Contingently false: something which is false, but it could have been true, e.g. "York is the capital of the UK"; you can only know it's false A POSTERIORI (contrast with CONTINGENTLY TRUE or NECESSARILY FALSE)

Contingently true: something which is true, but it could have been false, e.g. "London is the capital of the UK"; you can only know it's true A POSTERIORI (contrast with CONTINGENTLY FALSE or NECESSARILY TRUE)

Contradiction: a statement which makes two incompatible claims, or says something which cannot be true because it is a paradox e.g. "This wheel is not a wheel" or "Everything has a cause, but God is uncaused"

Corporeal: physical, material, consisting of matter such as atoms (contrast with INCORPOREAL / NON-CORPOREAL)

Cosmological argument: argument for the existence of God which suggests that the universe must have a cause, and that cause is God (see ARGUMENT FROM CONTINGENCY AND ARGUMENT FROM CAUSATION)

Counter-example: an example which disproves (or aims to disprove) a theory or ARGUMENT

Counter-intuitive: something which immediately seems wrong, contradicts common sense, or is paradoxical

Creationism: religious belief that God created the universe from nothing (and according to Christianity, that he did so in seven days)

Cyclic model: theory that the universe consists of a BIG BANG, then expansion, followed by contraction into a BIG CRUNCH, then another Big Bang. This continues infinitely into the past and future

Death by a thousand qualifications: a poor way of arguing; when a person is presented with evidence opposing their claim, they just alter their claim slightly to avoid the evidence, and they keep on doing this no matter how much evidence is presented to them (see INVISIBLE GARDENER)

Deductive argument: an argument which uses DEDUCTIVE REASONING. If the argument is VALID, then if premises are true, the conclusion is guaranteed to be true (contrast with ABDUCTIVE or INDUCTIVE ARGUMENTS)

Deductive reasoning: working something out using logic, so that the answer is guaranteed e.g. "Anna is a mother; all mothers are women; therefore Anna is a woman"; if the premises are true, we don't need to meet Anna to know that the conclusion is true (contrast with ABDUCTIVE or INDUCTIVE REASONING)

Denying the antecedent: a logical FALLACY which takes the form: "If P then Q. Not P. Therefore not Q." (contrast with MODUS TOLLENS) (see AFFIRMING THE CONSEQUENT)

Disjunction: an either-or statement such as "Either God exists, or he doesn't"

Divine action: actions performed by God, such as miracles or creating the Earth

Divine command: commands which come from God, e.g. the Ten Commandments, or when God commanded Abraham to kill his son Isaac

Divine revelation: God giving knowledge to humans through some sort of religious experience

Dualism: theory that two substances exist (MIND and MATTER)

Dubitable: able to be doubted (contrast with INDUBITABLE)

Eliminative materialism / eliminativism: theory that mental concepts such as QUALIA do not refer to anything and we should abandon such terminology in favour of something more scientific

Entail: in a DEDUCTIVE ARGUMENT, PREMISES must entail (logically ensure) the conclusion for the argument to be VALID; e.g. the premises "All crows are birds" and "All birds are animals" entail the conclusion "All crows are animals"

Epicurean hypothesis: criticism of ARGUMENTS FROM DESIGN, suggesting that an ordered system such as the universe can arise by random chance (named after Epicurus)

Epiphenomenalist dualism / epiphenomenalism: theory which attempts to solve the MIND-BODY INTERACTION PROBLEM by asserting that events in the brain and body produce events in the mind, but that those mental events are CAUSALLY INERT

Epistemic distance: idea that God is mysterious and doesn't interfere in our everyday lives too much, so that we aren't sure whether he exists (he does this so we act morally out of goodness, not just so we'll get into Heaven)

Eschatological: what happens at the end of life

Eschatological verification: notion that we can discover the truth of some propositions after death, e.g. it will become clear to us that Heaven exists

Eternal: God exists outside of time (he's timeless) (contrast with EVERLASTING)

Euthyphro dilemma: does God command something because it's good, or is it good just because God commands it?

Everlasting: God exists within time, but lasts forever (contrast with ETERNAL)

Evil: bad things such as suffering, pain and death – often separated into MORAL EVIL and NATURAL EVIL (see the PROBLEM OF EVIL)

Explicit premise: premises which are laid out in writing (contrast with IMPLICIT PREMISE)

Factually meaningful: a SYNTHETIC statement which reveals SUBSTANTIVE information about the world, and which can be VERIFIED (according to the LOGICAL POSITIVISTS) or which is open to being FALSIFIED (according to Flew)

Factually significant: a SYNTHETIC statement which reveals SUBSTANTIVE information about the world; not something which is merely TAUTOLOGICAL or ANALYTIC

Fallacies: mistaken or faulty reasoning

Fallacy of composition: assuming that because some things share a feature, that the group of them as a whole has that feature, e.g. "Every person has a mother, therefore there is someone who is the mother of everyone"

Fallible: capable of being false, e.g. a SYNTHETIC statement such as "there is a table in this room" could be false (contrast with INFALLIBLE)

False dilemma: a DISJUNCTION (either-or statement) where the two options being presented are not really the only two options, e.g. "Either you have children, or you despise children"

Falsification: proving something false; according to Flew, being open to falsification is what makes a religious statement FACTUALLY MEANINGFUL

Fine tuning argument: argument which is a compromise between CREATIONISM and evolutionary approaches, namely that God tweaked the universe so that life could develop and/or he continues to intervene in evolution

First cause: if everything is caused by something which happened before it, then there must be a first cause which caused everything else, i.e. God (see COSMOLOGICAL ARGUMENT)

First-person (immediate) access: I know my own thoughts because I have instant and effortless access to them; other people do not have this kind of access to my thoughts, even if they put me in a brain scanner

Folk psychology: general knowledge about the nature of the mind and the brain (which is not very scientific)

Free will: the ability to do what we choose, such as moving our limbs and making decisions

Functional duplicate: a person who is identical to me in the way they function, but they have different QUALIA (see INVERTED QUALIA) or no qualia at all (see ZOMBIES)

Functionalism: theory of mind which suggests that if something functions like a mind, then it *is* a mind – even if it is not a brain

Ghost in the machine: Ryle's reference to SUBSTANCE DUALISM (i.e. the brain is a machine, and dualism proposes that there is also a mystical thing called the mind within it)

Global scepticism: the process of doubting everything in order to build up beliefs which are certain and INFALLIBLE

God: often taken to mean a being that is OMNIPOTENT, OMNISCIENT, OMNIBENEVOLENT, and ETERNAL / EVERLASTING

Hard behaviourism: Hempel's theory that all descriptions of mental states can be reduced without loss of meaning into descriptions of behaviour, using the language of physics (see LOGICAL POSITIVISM)

Holy: people, places, or objects which are thought to encapsulate what is special and sacred about God, e.g. places of worship, crucifixes, sacred texts such as the Qur'an and Bible

Identity theory: see MIND-BRAIN-TYPE IDENTITY THEORY and MIND-BRAIN-TOKEN IDENTITY THEORY

If and only if: a way of stating NECESSARY AND SUFFICIENT CONDITIONS, e.g. "the game is over if and only if the referee says so". It is stronger than simply saying "if", because "the game is over if the referee says so" still allows that there can be other ways for the game to be over

Iff: shortened form of IF AND ONLY IF

Immanent: God exists within the material world (contrast with TRANSCENDENT) (see OMNIPRESENT and PANTHEISM)

Immaterial: non-physical and not made of matter (contrast with MATERIAL)

Immaterialism: the MONIST theory that only minds and their ideas exist, i.e. nothing physical exists (contrast with DUALISM or MATERIALISM)

Immortal: a being is immortal if it never dies or cannot die

Immutability: the suggestion that God cannot or does not change

Implicit premise: an assumption or premise which is not laid out in writing, but exists in the mind of the author and/or reader; also called a suppressed premise or implied premise (contrast with EXPLICIT PREMISE)

Incommunicable attributes of God: attributes which human beings cannot have, and which belong to God alone, e.g. TRANSCENDENCE, OMNIPOTENCE, OMNISCIENCE (contrast with COMMUNICABLE ATTRIBUTES)

Inconsistent triad: three incompatible statements such as "God is OMNIPOTENT", "God is OMNIBENEVOLENT", and "Evil exists in the world". One of the statements must be abandoned or modified to avoid the contradiction (see the PROBLEM OF EVIL)

Incorporeal: non-physical, IMMATERIAL (contrast with CORPOREAL)

Indivisibility argument: see ARGUMENT FROM INDIVISIBILITY

Indubitable: something which cannot be doubted; it is 100% certain (contrast with DUBITABLE)

Inductive argument: an ARGUMENT which uses INDUCTIVE REASONING. If the premises are true, the conclusion is likely to be true (contrast with ABDUCTIVE or DEDUCTIVE ARGUMENTS)

Inductive reasoning: working something out based on evidence or experience, but the conclusion is never certain, e.g. no people have ever had blue skin, so it's fairly safe to conclude that the next person I meet will not have blue skin (contrast with ABDUCTIVE or DEDUCTIVE REASONING)

Ineffable: incapable of being described in words – God or qualia may be ineffable

Infallible: impossible for it to be false (contrast with FALLIBLE)

Inference to the best explanation: arguing that a particular theory is the best explanation for the data, compared to other theories (see ABDUCTIVE REASONING)

Inference: to work logically from PREMISES towards a CONCLUSION

Infinite regress: something which goes on and on for ever

Intelligent design: things in the world such as the human eye are so complex that they cannot have come about by evolution alone; they must have been designed by an intelligent being, i.e. God (see ARGUMENT FROM DESIGN)

Intentional thought: thoughts which possess INTENTIONALITY (do not use the term "intentional thoughts" to mean thoughts which one has on purpose!)

Intentionality: a mental event which represents something or has some content; one can't just remember or hope – one has to remember *an event* or hope *that something is the case*

Interaction problem: see MIND-BODY INTERACTION or MIND-BODY PROBLEM

Intermediate conclusion: a CONCLUSION that can be drawn from PREMISES, but is not the end of the argument (one or more conclusions will follow)

Intermingling thesis: Descartes' claim that although the mind and body are distinct SUBSTANCES, they are intermingled in the human body so that we *feel* pain rather than merely observing it

Intrinsic: essential; a vital property of something

Introspection: searching within one's own mind; considering one's own thoughts

Introspective access: I can access my thoughts easily merely by thinking about them; I am NON-INFERENTIALLY aware of them

Intuition: a feeling of being correct about something; it may be more than just a gut feeling, such as the grasping of a SELF-EVIDENT truth

Invalid argument: an argument where the CONCLUSION is not ENTAILED by the PREMISES, e.g. John is a man, therefore John likes sandwiches

Inverted qualia: a FUNCTIONAL DUPLICATE may be functionally identical to me, but what he calls a high-pitched sound, I would call a low-pitched sound; what he calls blue, I would call orange; what he calls pain, I would call pleasure

Invisible gardener: thought experiment by Flew: there is a gardener who is invisible, undetectable, silent, etc. to the point where he is no different from a non-existent gardener (see DEATH BY A THOUSAND QUALIFICATIONS)

Irenaean theodicy: theory that evil exists on Earth because suffering develops our souls and prepares us for Heaven (see VALE OF SOUL-MAKING)

Judeo-Christian: referring to Jewish and Christian people or beliefs

Kalam argument: DEDUCTIVE COSMOLOGICAL ARGUMENT which states that everything with a beginning has a cause, and since the universe had a beginning, it must have a cause – and only an uncaused, IMMATERIAL and ETERNAL being such as God could have created the universe

Language game: term used by Wittgenstein to show that the meaning of a word varies according to the way it is used in a sentence; it is meaningful if others within the same language "game" understand it

Leibniz's Law (of identity): if A is the same thing as B, then whatever is true of A is also true of B

Location problem: argument in favour of DUALISM which states that we know the location of the brain (in our heads), but we don't know the location of the mind as it's NON-PHYSICAL, therefore they are different things

Logic: working something out in a formal, pre-defined way so as to not make any mistakes

Logical behaviourism: see BEHAVIOURISM

Logical form: the structure of an argument, revealed by replacing all the subjects and PREDICATES with variables, e.g. X is a Y, All Y's are Z's, therefore X is a Z

Logical positivism: a logical approach towards philosophy which asserts the VERIFICATION PRINCIPLE as a criterion of meaningfulness

Logically impossible: something which cannot be conceived of or imagined, e.g. a 3-sided square, or that 2 + 3 = 10 (contrast with LOGICALLY POSSIBLE or ACTUALLY IMPOSSIBLE)

Logically possible: something which can be conceived of and imagined, even if it isn't possible in reality, e.g. for a man to run a marathon in 4 seconds (contrast with LOGICALLY IMPOSSIBLE or ACTUALLY POSSIBLE)

Logically private: my thoughts are necessarily known only to me; even if I am put into a brain scanner, others will not know exactly what my thoughts are

Mary's black and white room: thought experiment by Jackson: Mary has always lived in a black and white room, and has become a theoretical expert on the physics of colour vision – when she sees colour for the first time, will she learn anything new?

Masked man fallacy: a fallacy stemming from the misuse of LEIBNIZ'S LAW; one assumes that the *appearance* of different qualities means that there are two different things (when in fact they are the same thing), e.g. one assumes Superman is not Clark Kent because Superman can fly and Clark Kent cannot

Material: physical; made of matter (contrast with IMMATERIAL)

Materialism: theory that the only SUBSTANCE in existence is physical matter (contrast with SUBSTANCE DUALISM or IMMATERIALISM)

Matter: physical substances made of atoms, elements, etc

Mental causation: the notion that mental states can cause physical behaviours (see MIND-BODY INTERACTION)

Metaphysical freedom: see FREE WILL

Metaphysically impossible: see LOGICALLY IMPOSSIBLE

Metaphysically possible: see LOGICALLY POSSIBLE

Metaphysics: the branch of philosophy which investigates things that are "beyond physics", i.e. the nature of reality, what exists, and what it is like

Methodological behaviourism: theory that science should concern itself with what is publicly accessible (i.e. behaviour) rather than inner mental states

Mind states: thinking, hoping, knowing, feeling sad, happy, hungry, pain, etc

Mind-body interaction: theories which attempt to explain how the mind and the brain/body interact

Mind-body problem: problem for DUALIST theories of mind – they need to explain how the NON-PHYSICAL mind and the physical brain/body interact

Mind-brain-token identity theory: the stronger form of IDENTITY THEORY which claims that mental states that are ONTOLOGICALLY REDUCIBLE to physical properties i.e. a particular type of mental state (e.g. pain) is matched to various different TOKENS of neuronal firing patterns

Mind-brain-type identity theory: the weaker form of IDENTITY THEORY which claims that mental states are ONTOLOGICALLY REDUCIBLE to physical properties i.e. a particular type of mental state (e.g. pain) is matched exactly to a particular TYPE of neuronal firing pattern

Mindedness: the quality of having a mind

Modus ponens: a VALID ARGUMENT which "affirms the ANTECEDENT"; it takes the LOGICAL FORM "If P then Q. P. Therefore, Q"

Modus tollens: a VALID ARGUMENT which "denies the CONSEQUENT"; it takes the LOGICAL FORM "If P then Q. Not Q. Therefore, not P"

Monism: theory that only one type of substance exists – MATERIALISM and IMMATERIALISM are both monist theories (contrast with DUALISM)

Monochromatic: black and white (no colours)

Monotheism: belief in a single God (contrast with POLYTHEISM)

Moral evil: suffering caused by humans, e.g. torture, human sacrifice, war, murder, violence, rape

Multiple realisability: the notion that a particular mental state (e.g. fear) can be manifested in various different ways (different brain states or different types of behaviour)

Mystery: as an attribute of God, mystery means that he only reveals particular information to humans (see EPISTEMIC DISTANCE)

Naïve behaviourism: a dismissive term for HARD BEHAVIOURISM

Natural evil: suffering caused by natural events or natural disasters, e.g. cancer, famine, plagues, earthquakes, tsunamis, avalanches

Natural theology: coming to understand the nature of God through everyday experience and/or REASON alone (not through understanding sacred texts) (contrast with REVEALED THEOLOGY)

Necessarily false: something which is false, and it could not have been true, e.g. "triangles have 5 sides"; you can know it's false A PRIORI (contrast with NECESSARILY TRUE or CONTINGENTLY FALSE)

Necessarily true: something which is true, and it could not have been false, e.g. "triangles have 3 sides"; you can know it's true A PRIORI (contrast with NECESSARILY FALSE or CONTINGENTLY TRUE)

Necessary and sufficient conditions: condition(s) which are needed, and are enough to satisfy something, e.g. having a teaching qualification is both necessary and sufficient to allow you to be a teacher (see IF AND ONLY IF)

Necessary being: a being which must necessarily exist – it would be a contradiction for it not to exist. ONTOLOGICAL ARGUMENTS and some COSMOLOGICAL ARGUMENTS suggest that God is a necessary being

Necessary conditions: a condition which is needed in order to do something, e.g. it is necessary to be conscious in order to pass a degree – but it is not SUFFICIENT (i.e. you need more than just consciousness)

Neurochemical: chemicals in the brain

Neurones: cells in the brain and spinal cord

Non-cognitivism: theory that when we make religious statements such as "God lives in all of us" we are not (merely) articulating our beliefs; religious statements do not need to be VERIFIABLE or FALSIFIABLE in order to be meaningful (contrast with COGNITIVISM)

Non-corporeal: non-physical, IMMATERIAL (contrast with CORPOREAL)

Non-inferential: something which does not need to be worked out based on other facts; it is SELF-EVIDENT

Non-physical: things which are not made up of electrons, atoms (etc); the mind or God may be non-physical

Non-reductive: a theory is non-reductive if it suggests that one entity cannot be reduced to another (e.g. PROPERTY DUALISM is a form of non-reductive MONISM because mental events cannot be reduced to physical events)

Noumena: things which exist but are beyond human sensory perception

Numerical identity: something is numerically the same as itself; I am numerically the same person I was at birth (I haven't duplicated myself) but I am not QUALITATIVELY the same, as my features have changed

Numinous: holy, spiritual, or supernatural

Occasionalism: theory which attempts to solve the MIND-BODY INTERACTION problem by saying that God serves as the link between mind and body: God notices that my body is feeling thirsty, and tells my mind to think "I'm thirsty", then he tells my brain to tell my hand to reach out and pick up the drink!

Ockham's (or Occam's) razor: the idea that non-essential elements of a theory should be removed; the best explanation is the simplest one which does not rely on supernatural entities when they aren't required

Omnibenevolent: all-loving; totally good

Omnipotent: all-powerful; having the power to do anything

Omnipresent: existing everywhere in the universe at once

Omniscient: all-seeing and all-knowing; the ability to see and know everything that is going on in the universe at once, and have infinite knowledge

Ontological argument: an A PRIORI argument which tries to show that the very definition of God is proof that he exists, e.g. God is (by definition) perfect, existence is a perfection, so God exists

Ontological reduction: when the claims or events in one domain refer exactly to claims or events within another domain (e.g. mental events are exactly the same thing as BRAIN STATES) – however we may use the two sets of terms differently (contrast with ANALYTIC REDUCTION)

Ontology: the study of existence, reality and the nature of being, i.e. trying to find out what exists

Other minds: the minds of other people (humans)

P: just as *x* and *y* are often used in mathematical formulae, P and Q are often used in philosophical ARGUMENTS presented in STANDARD FORM (potentially any letters can be used though); P often stands for a PROPOSITION

Pantheism: belief that God and the universe are the same thing: God *is* the universe (contrast with MONOTHEISM) (see OMNIPRESENT and IMMANENT)

Paradox of the stone: can God make a stone too heavy for him to lift? Whether he either can't make it, or can't lift it, there's something he can't do, so he's not OMNIPOTENT

Paradox: a contradiction or something which simply cannot be true, e.g. "my brother exists, but he doesn't exist"; 1 + 2 = 5; "Trevor is a married bachelor"

Parallelism: theory which attempts to solve the MIND-BODY INTERACTION problem by saying that God keeps my mind and brain always acting in parallel (like two clocks which independently keep the same time); my mind and brain *appear* to interact, but they don't

Parsimonious: a theory is parsimonious if it is "economical" with the things it proposes (it doesn't suggest any extra or unnecessary parts) (see OCKHAM'S RAZOR)

Pascal's wager: if you believe in God and he exists, you get into Heaven, (and if he doesn't exist then nothing happens after death), whereas if you don't believe in God, then if he exists you'll go to Hell (and if he doesn't exist then still nothing happens). So you should believe in God just in case he exists

Personal continuity: the idea that my identity / personality / mind / soul could continue elsewhere (e.g. in Heaven) in another form, and I would still be me

Phenomenology: the study of conscious experiences from a first-personal point of view (see QUALIA)

Philosophical behaviourism: see BEHAVIOURISM

Physical evil: see NATURAL EVIL

Physical universe: all the things within the universe which are made up of physical particles, from electrons, to tables, to stars and galaxies

Physicalism: theory of mind which suggests that that everything in the universe is physical or SUPERVENES on the physical (i.e. there are no NON-PHYSICAL SUBSTANCES)

Physically possible: see ACTUALLY POSSIBLE

Physico-theological: Kant suggests that arguments from design should be called physico-theological arguments, as they move from physical evidence towards a theological conclusion

Piety: goodness / holiness

Polytheism: belief in multiple Gods, e.g. the God of death, the God of the ocean, the God of love (contrast with MONOTHEISM)

Possible worlds: other ways in which reality could have turned out (see ALL POSSIBLE WORLDS)

Precision: getting the wording of your exam answers exactly correct and not "waffling"

Predicate: a property of something; part of a PROPOSITION or claim which describes the SUBJECT, e.g. in the sentence "The table is square", "is square" is the predicate

Premise: a claim or PROPOSITION which forms part of an ARGUMENT, e.g. "Tyler is a man" and "All men are human" are premises which ENTAIL the CONCLUSION "Tyler is human"

Principle of sufficient reason: claim that every CONTINGENT fact must have an adequate explanation of why it turned out that way, rather than some other way (e.g. there must be a reason why grass is green, not blue)

Problem of counting souls: it's usually assumed that there's one soul for each person, but there could be thousands and we'd not realise it, as we can't know it through sense experience

Problem of evil: if God is OMNIPOTENT, OMNISCIENT and OMNIBENEVOLENT, then why does evil exist in the world? Why doesn't God stop it? (see INCONSISTENT TRIAD)

Problem of other minds: a problem for DUALISM: we can't be truly certain that other people have minds, because a mind is something non-physical

Process theology: a form of THEOLOGY which suggests that God has a TEMPORAL aspect and an ATEMPORAL aspect, and that God is not OMNIPOTENT in that he controls absolutely everything, but he does exert control ("persuasion") over the universe in general

Property dualism: MONIST theory that only one SUBSTANCE exists (matter), but brains have two *properties* – physical and mental properties; MENTAL EVENTS are not SUPERVENIENT upon nor REDUCIBLE to physical events

Proposition: a statement of fact (or which *attempts* to be factual) such as "Bachelors are unmarried", "There are four lights", or "Cows make milk"

Propositional knowledge: factual knowledge; knowing that something is the case, e.g. knowing that Paris is the capital of France, or that Debbie is wearing blue socks today (contrast with ACQUAINTANCE KNOWLEDGE or ABILITY KNOWLEDGE)

Pseudo-proposition: something which makes grammatical sense, but is not VERIFIABLE (according to LOGICAL POSITIVISTS) e.g. "love is a chasm silently echoing in the darkness"

Q: see P

Qua: "as relating to"; (see the ARGUMENT FROM DESIGN QUA PURPOSE and the ARGUMENT FROM DESIGN QUA REGULARITY)

Quale / qualia: the unique way a feeling feels to an individual, e.g. the smell of flowers, the taste of a hot dog, the feeling of terror

Qualitative identity: something is qualitatively the same as another object with the exact same features; two pens can be just like one another if they are the same size, thickness, colour (etc) but they are not NUMERICALLY the same because there are two of them; they are the same TYPE but different TOKENS (see TYPE-TOKEN DISTINCTION)

Question-begging: see BEGGING THE QUESTION

Reason: logical thinking as a way of acquiring knowledge (as opposed to experience)

Reductionism: making something simpler or easier to understand, or translating it into different (easier) terminology (see ONTOLOGICAL REDUCTION and ANALYTIC REDUCTION)

Redundancy: when something is not needed for a theory or argument to make its point or be successful (see PARSIMONY)

Regularities of co-presence: term Swinburne uses to refer to amazing physical things such as the human eye, how well-adapted animals are to their environment, and the ways plants and animals reproduce

Regularities of succession: term Swinburne uses to refer to cause-and-effect relationships such as the way planets orbit stars, and the way a ball thrown up in the air falls to the ground again

Religious concepts: notions such as God, TRANSCENDENCE, OMNIPOTENCE, Heaven, or miracles

Religious language: words, concepts and propositions which are used to refer to religious things

Religious propositions: statements which make religious claims or state religious beliefs, such as "God is OMNISCIENT" or "There is life after death"

Revealed theology: coming to understand the nature of God through studying sacred texts (not through everyday experience or REASON alone) (contrast with NATURAL THEOLOGY)

Revelation: when God reveals himself to people, either by appearing "in person" or via holy beings such as angels; these revelations may be written down to form part of a SACRED TEXT (see REVEALED THEOLOGY)

Sacred text: a religious book such as the Bible or Qur'an

Scepticism: doubting a particular field of study, or more than one field of study (see GLOBAL SCEPTICISM)

Secular: non-religious

Self-evident: beliefs or PROPOSITIONS which can be known to be true simply by considering them, e.g. that 3 is larger than 2

Slippery slope argument: a weak way of arguing involving the claim that if we permit a small (negative) act, it will lead on to greater (negative) acts, e.g. if we allow children to buy lottery tickets, it will lead to them becoming gambling addicts

Soft behaviourism: strongest form of behaviourism by Ryle, that all descriptions of mental states are descriptions of behavioural dispositions, using ordinary language

Solipsism: the theory that I am the only mind in existence

Sophistry: using clever but faulty arguments to deceive or trick opponents

Soul: most THEISTS believe the soul to be the non-physical and IMMORTAL essence of a human (and maybe an animal)

Sound argument: an argument which follows a VALID FORM, and the PREMISES are true (therefore the CONCLUSION must also be true)

Standard form: a way of setting out ARGUMENTS, either by numbering or bullet pointing the PREMISES and CONCLUSION ("C" may be used for the conclusion)

Subject: the item or person that a PROPOSITION is about, e.g. in the sentence "The table is square", the subject is "the table" (see PREDICATE)

Substance dualism: dualist theory that two SUBSTANCES exist: mind and MATTER; the mind and the brain are different things

Substance: a word used to mean "type of thing" which can exist by itself – e.g. there may be two substances, the mental and the physical

Substantive: meaningful, significant truths about the world; truths which are not ANALYTIC, TAUTOLOGICAL, or mathematical; substantive facts are FACTUALLY SIGNIFICANT

Sufficient conditions: conditions which are enough for something, e.g. having run your own café is enough to qualify you to do the washing up in a different café, but it is not NECESSARY (i.e. you don't *need* to have run your own café in order to do the washing up)

Super-Spartans: a group of people in ancient Greece who did not show any outward signs of pain, even though they felt it

Supervenience: supervenient properties depend on something else: if the mind supervenes on the brain then there cannot be a change in mental events without some corresponding change in the physical brain

Syllogism: a three line ARGUMENT consisting of two PREMISES and a CONCLUSION, often including a major premise ("All X's are Y"), a minor premise ("This is an X"), and a conclusion ("Therefore this is a Y")

Synthetically false: a proposition which is false, but its falsity cannot be known simply by understanding the meanings of the words – you also need to know something about the world, e.g. "Prince Charles has two daughters" (contrast with SYNTHETICALLY TRUE or ANALYTICALLY FALSE)

Synthetically true: a proposition which is true, but its truth cannot be known simply by understanding the meanings of the words – you also need to know something about the world, e.g. "Prince Charles has two sons" (contrast with SYNTHETICALLY FALSE or ANALYTICALLY TRUE)

Tautology: a PROPOSITION or argument which is just repeating itself, e.g. "A hippo is a hippo" or "God exists, therefore God is in existence"

Teleological argument: an argument which refers to the purpose of something (e.g. the universe was designed for a purpose) (see ARGUMENT FROM DESIGN)

Temporal: relating to time or occurring within time (see EVERLASTING) (contrast with ATEMPORAL)

Theism: belief in one or more Gods

Theodicy: an explanation or justification of God's actions, such as explaining why an OMNIPOTENT, OMNISCIENT, OMNIBENEVOLENT God would allow there to be EVIL in the world (see the PROBLEM OF EVIL)

Theology: the study of God from a religious perspective (as opposed to a philosophical perspective, which questions God much more readily)

Token: see TYPE-TOKEN DISTINCTION and NUMERICAL IDENTITY

Trademark argument: Descartes' argument that because he has the idea of a perfect God, this idea must have come from God himself, who put the idea into Descartes' mind to let him know who made him (this is based on the CAUSAL ADEQUACY PRINCIPLE)

Transcendent: God exists outside of or beyond the universe (contrast with IMMANENT)

Truth-apt: something that is truth-apt has the possibility of being true e.g. "Today is Tuesday" is truth-apt, whereas "Hello, how are you?" and "Today is a wonderful day!" are not truth-apt (see TRUTH-VALUE)

Truth-value: whether a PROPOSITION is true or false, e.g. "The author of this book owns a blue car" has a truth-value because it's either true or false, whereas "Marmite is revolting" doesn't have a truth-value – it's just an opinion

Turing test: two people and a test subject (usually a computer) have a text-based conversation on a screen, and if the people can't tell who is the other person and who is the computer, then the computer has passed the test and it has a mind

Type-token distinction: two chairs which look the same are the same type of chair, but different tokens (see QUALITATIVE IDENTITY and NUMERICAL IDENTITY)

Unity: an attribute of God: that he forms a complete whole, and there is only one of him

Unmoved mover: Aristotle claims that God is the FIRST CAUSE of everything in the universe; he set everything in motion, but nothing moved him (see COSMOLOGICAL ARGUMENT)

Vale of soul-making: Hick calls Earth the "vale of soul-making", as he claims that our lives of suffering here prepare our souls for Heaven

Valid argument: an argument where the CONCLUSION is ENTAILED by the premises, i.e. if the premises are true, the conclusion *must* be true too (but if the premises are false, the conclusion might be false) e.g. "All fish are blue, Nemo is a fish, therefore Nemo is orange" is valid (see SOUND ARGUMENT)

Valid form: an argument which is constructed so as to make it VALID, even when its PROPOSITIONS, SUBJECTS and PREDICATES are replaced by letters, e.g. "All P is Q, Q is R, therefore P is R" is a valid form

Veracious / veracity: truth; when put forward as an attribute of God, it means that he *is* the truth

Verifiable in principle: knowing what it would take to prove the truth of a statement (even if that evidence could never practically be gathered) e.g. the statement "there is a kitten orbiting Jupiter" would be proven true if we checked Jupiter's orbit and found a kitten

Verification principle: rule put forward by VERIFICATIONISTS such as Ayer, that a statement is only FACTUALLY MEANINGFUL if it is ANALYTICALLY TRUE or it is VERIFIABLE IN PRINCIPLE (see VIENNA CIRCLE)

Verificationism: theory which puts forward the VERIFICATION PRINCIPLE

Vienna Circle: a group of LOGICAL POSITIVISTS working together in Vienna, Austria during the 1920s and 30s

Zombie: a being which looks and acts exactly like a normal human being, but inside it has no mind (see FUNCTIONAL DUPLICATE)

Index

A posteriori: 9, 48, 62-71

A priori: 9, 48, 55-61, 72-73, 82

Abductive argument: 8, **12-13**, 14, 62, 72, 121-123

Ability / acquaintance knowledge: 34-35, 117, 144

Actually possible / impossible: 104, 106

Ad hominem: 19

Affirming the consequent: 16-17

Al-Ghazali: 72

Analytic reduction: 125, 129, 132

Analytic truths / falsehoods: 9, 56, 81-83, 125

Analytical behaviourism: see *Behaviourism*

Anomalous monism: see *Identity theory*

Anselm, St.: 22-24, 55-56, **57-59**

Antecedents and consequents: 10, 16-17

Aquinas, St. Thomas: 33-34, 37, 47, 58, 69, **70-71**, **75-76**

Argument from analogy: **62-66**, 67, 87-88, 91, **121-123**

Argument from causation: 24, 46, **68-75**

Argument from conceivability: 27-28, 56, 98, **101-105**, 106, 115, **131-2**

Argument from contingency: 60-61, 69, **75-78**

Argument from design: 62-68

Argument from design qua purpose: 62-66

Argument from design qua regularity: 62, **66-68**

Argument from indivisibility: 97-98, **105-107**, 131

Argument from introspection: 96, **113**, 127

Argument from motion: 23-4, 69, **70-71**

Aristotle: 37, 47, **68-70**, 71

Arnauld, Antoine: 102

Aseity: 30

Atemporality: see *Eternal*

Atheism: 50-51, 55, 57, 75, 81, 84, 88-90, 109

Attacking a straw man: **18-19**, 25, 42, 63, 97

Attributes of God: 23-4, **30-54**, 57-61, 64-65, 67-79, 83, 86, 88, 108-109

Augustine, St.: 38, 47, 51

Averroes: 41

Ayer, A. J.: **81-3**, 84

Begging the question: **15**, 57, 98, 100, 102, 107, 116, 131

Behaviourism: 13, 95, 96, 103, 112, 114, 119, 121-123, **124-128**, 137, 139

Big Bang: 67, 69-70, 72-73, 76

Blik: 90-92

Block, Ned: 138, 140

Burden of proof: 55

Category mistake: **17-18**, 99-100, 126

Causal adequacy principle: 74-5

Causal inertness / closure (of the physical universe): 100, 110-113

Chalmers, David: 113-116

Chinese mind / head: 138-140

Chinese room: 137-140

Churchland, Patricia: 118-119, **134-136**

Churchland, Paul: 117-119, **134-136**
Circular justification: 15
Cognitivism / non-cognitivism: **80**, 81-84, 87-92
Communicable attributes of God: 31
Conceivability argument: see *Argument from conceivability*
Contingent being: see *Necessary being*
Contradictions: 11, **15-16**, 18, 33, 41-43, 47-49, 56-57, 59-60, 69, 71, 76, 78-80
Cosmological arguments: 62, **68-78**
Cyclic model: 70
Death by a thousand qualifications: 33, **88**
Deductive argument: 8, 10, **11**, 13-14, 46, 48, 55-61, 72-73
Dennett, Daniel: 118-9, **133-136**
Denying the antecedent: 10, **17**
Design arguments: 62-68
Descartes, René: 27, 56-57, **59-60**, 69, 73-75, **96-111**, 132
Divine action: see *Problem of divine action*
Dualism: see *Property dualism* or *Substance dualism*
Eliminative materialism: 95, 118-9, 123-4, **133-136**
Epicurean hypothesis: 64-65
Epicurus: 48, 64-65
Epiphenomenalism: 108, **111-113**
Epistemic distance: 54
Eschatological verification: 83, **84-86**
Eternal: 30, 32-33, 36-38, **39-41**, 61, 68, 72-74, 76
Euthyphro dilemma: 5, 32, 38, **43-45**, 46
Everlasting: 30, 35-37, **39-41**, 61, 68
Evil: 5, 25, 30, 32-37, 39, 43-45, **46-54**, 65, 69, 88, 101
Fallacies:
- Ad hominem: 19
- Affirming the consequent: 16-17
- Attacking a straw man: **18-19**, 25, 42, 63, 97
- Begging the question: **15**, 57, 98, 100, 102, 107, 116, 131
- Category mistake: **17-18**, 99-100, 126
- Circular justification: 15
- Contradictions: 11, **15-16**, 18, 33, 41-43, 47-49, 56-57, 59-60, 69, 71, 76, 78-80
- Denying the antecedent: 10, **17**
- Fallacy of composition: 18, 69
- False dilemma: **16**, 52, 61, 73
- Masked man fallacy: **17**, 27-28, **99**, 100, 102, 107, 131-132
- Slippery slope argument: 19
Fallacy of composition: 18, 69
False dilemma: **16**, 52, 61, 73
Falsification: 81, 83, **87-92**
Fine tuning argument: 65, 88
First cause: 24, 46, **68-76**
First-person (immediate) access: 96, 98, 134, 136
Flew, Antony: 52-53, **87-92**
Folk psychology: 118-9, **134-136**
Free will: 5, 32, 36-37, 40-41, 49, **51-53**, 67, 88, 113
Free will defence: 51-53
Functionalism: 95, 103, 119, 123, **137-140**
Gaunilo: 58

Ghost in the machine: 99, 124
God: 9, 16, 20, 22-25, **29-92**, 108-109, 112, 125
Hard behaviourism: 103, 123, 125-128
Hare, R. M.: 90-91
Hempel, Carl: 103, 124-127
Hick, John: 53-54, 84-86
Hume, David: 49, 56, 62-66, 69, 70, 76, 78, 118
Identity theory: 95, 119, 123, 126, **129-132**, 133, 139
Immanence: 30, 32, 35, 39-40
Immutability: 30, 32-36, 38, 45, 72-74
Incommunicable attributes of God: 31
Inconsistent triad: 47-48
Indivisibility argument: 97-98, **105-107**, 131
Inductive argument: 8, 12-14, 48-49, 62, 68
Ineffability: 30, 58, 95-96, 115, 136, 139
Infallibility: 95, 98, 122
Inference to the best explanation: 8, **12-14**, 62, 72, 121-123, 135
Infinite regress: 70-71, 74
Intentionality: 95-6, 133
Interaction problem: **107-113**, 124, 128, 131
Intermingling thesis: **97**, 100, 103, 109
Introspection: 95-96, 113, 116, 127, 136
Invalid argument: 11
Inverted qualia: 134-136, 139
Invisible gardener: 87-88
Irenaean theodicy: 53-54
Irenaeus: 53-54
Jackson, Frank: 18, 116-119, 139
Kalam argument: 69, 72-73
Kant, Immanuel: 57, 60-61, 65, 67
Kenny, Anthony: 37
Kierkegaard, Søren: 44
Kretzmann, Norman: 35-6
Language game: 80-81
Leibniz, Gottfried Wilhelm: 17, 27-28, 53, 69, **77-78**, 97, 99-101, 104-105, 131
Leibniz's Law (of identity): 17, 27-28, **97**, 99-101, 104-105, 131
Lewis, David: 117
Location problem: 132
Logical positivism: **81-83**, 84, 86-87, 125 (also see *Verificationism*)
Logically possible / impossible: 33-34, 36, 42, 52, 60-61, 79, 88, 101
Mackie, J. L.: 48, 52-53, 68, 70, 76
Malcolm, Norman: 56, **60-61**
Mary's black and white room: 18, **116-119**, 139
Masked man fallacy: **17**, 27-28, **99**, 100, 102, 107, 131-132
Mavrodes, George: 41-42
Metaphysics of mind: 93-140
Metaphysics of God: 29-92
Mind-body interaction problem: **107-113**, 124, 128, 131
Mind-brain-token identity theory: see *Identity theory*
Mind-brain-type identity theory: see *Identity theory*
Mitchell, Basil: 90, **91-92**
Modus ponens: 10, 16
Modus tollens: 10, 17
Monism: 94, 113, 123-136
Moral evil: 47-54
Multiple realisability: 123, 126-128, 130-132, 137, 139

Natural evil: 47-54
Necessary being: 58, 60-61, 69, 75-78
Non-cognitivism: 80, 90
Occasionalism: 108-109, 112
Ockham's razor: 45, 70, 109, 112, 122 (also see *Parsimony*)
Omnibenevolence: 30, 32, 34-36, **37-39**, 43-54, 61, 65, 67-68, 76
Omnipotence: 30, 32, **33-34**, 37, 39-43, 45-54, 59, 61, 65, 67-68, 74, 76, 78-79, 88, 108
Omnipresence: 30, 35, 39
Omniscience: 30, 32, **34-37**, 39-41, 48-51, 59, 61, 67-69, 74, 78, 86
Ontological arguments: 22-24, 46, **55-61**
Ontological reduction: 123, 129, 132-133
Other minds: 13, **119-123**, 128
Paley, William: 62-66
Pantheism: 39 (also see *Omnipresence*)
Paradox of the stone: 32-33, **41-43**, 46
Parallelism: 109, 112
Parsimony: 70, 109, 112, 124, 130-131 (also see *Ockham's razor*)
Phenomenology: 95, 113, 117-118, 122, 124
Physicalism: 27-28, 94-100, 102-103, 107-108, 114-119, **123-136**, 137, 139
Plantinga, Alvin: 51-53
Plato: 37, **43-45**
Precision (in essays): 21-23, 25, 27-28
Predicate: 9, 60
Princess of Bohemia, Elisabeth: 110, 113
Principle of sufficient reason: 77-78
Problem of counting souls: 100
Problem of divine action: 32-33, 38, 40
Problem of evil: 5, 25, 30, 32, 34, 37, 39, **46-54**
Problem of free will: 5, 32, 36-37, 40-41, 49, **51-53**, 67, 88, 113
Problem of other minds: **119-123**, 128
Process theology: 50
Property dualism: 26, 94, 106-108, 113-116
Propositional knowledge: 34-35, 117
Putnam, Hilary: 127-128, **131-132**
Qualia: 95-96, 98, 100, 113-119, 123-124, 132-136, 138-140
Reductionism: 123, 125, 129, 132-133
Redundancy (in essays): 23-24
Regularities of co-presence: 62, 64-66,
Regularities of succession: 62, 66-68
Religious language: 79-92
Russell, Bertrand: 55, 57, 69-70, 76, 78
Ryle, Gilbert: 17, 99, 120, 122, 124-128
Sartre, Jean-Paul: 50
Savage, C. W.: 42-43
Scepticism: 59
Schopenhauer, Arthur: 57
Searle, John: 137-140
Smart, J. J. C.: 129-130
Socrates: 11, 19, **43-45**, 47
Soft behaviourism: 123, 125, 127-128
Solipsism: 119-120, 123
Soul: 49, 53-54, 81, 83, 85-86, 88-89, 97, 100, 128

Soul-making defence: 53-54
Specification: 5, 6, 46, **141-146**
Standard form: 8, 24
Substance dualism: 26-27, 94-95, **96-113**, 116, 119, 124, 128, 137, 139
Super-Spartans: 121, 127-128
Supervenience: 114, 123-124, 129, 133, 137
Swinburne, Richard: 62, 66-68
Synthetic truths / falsehoods: 56
Teleological arguments: 62-68
Temporality: see *Everlasting*
Theodicies: 49, 51-54
Token identity theory: see *Identity theory*
Trademark argument: 74-5
Transcendence: 30-3, 35, 38, 40
Turing test: 137
Type identity theory: see *Identity theory*
Type-token distinction: 130
Unmoved mover: 23-4, **69**, 70-71
Vale of soul-making: 53-4
Verificationism / verification principle: **81-86**, 122, 124-5, 127
Vienna Circle: **81-83**, 124-5
Wittgenstein, Ludwig: 80-81, 120, 128
Zombies: 112, **114-116**, 119, 121-122, 136, 139

Printed in Great Britain
by Amazon

29575562R00099